How to Get Into a Military Service Academy

How to Get Into a Military Service Academy

A Step-by-Step Guide to Getting Qualified, Nominated, and Appointed

Michael Singer Dobson

ROWMAN & LITTLEFIELD
Lanham • Boulder • New York • London

Published by Rowman & Littlefield
A wholly owned subsidiary of
The Rowman & Littlefield Publishing Group, Inc.
4501 Forbes Boulevard, Suite 200, Lanham, Maryland 20706
www.rowman.com

Unit A, Whitacre Mews, 26-34 Stannary Street, London SE11 4AB

British Library Cataloguing in Publication Information Available

Library of Congress Cataloging-in-Publication Data
Dobson, Michael Singer.
  How to get into a military service academy : a step-by-step guide to getting
qualified, nominated, and appointed / Michael Singer Dobson.
      pages cm
  Includes bibliographical references and index.
  ISBN 978-1-4422-4314-9 (cloth : alk. paper) — ISBN 978-1-4422-4315-6
(electronic) 1. United States Military Academy—Admission. 2. United
States Air Force Academy—Admission. 3. United States Naval Academy—
Admission. I. Title.
  U410.Q1D62 2015
  355.0071'173—dc23

2015019469

Printed in the United States of America

This book is dedicated with pride, love, and admiration to my son:

Cadet James Dobson
West Point Class of 2018

Contents

Tables   xv

Preface   xvii

How to Use This Book   xxi

1   ABOUT THE ACADEMIES   1

    United States Military Academy (West Point)   3
    United States Naval Academy   4
    United States Coast Guard Academy   5
    United States Merchant Marine Academy   7
    United States Air Force Academy   9
    United States Senior Military Colleges/ROTC   9
    Preparatory Schools   10
    Graduate Schools   11
    Which Academy Should You Choose?   11

2   IS A SERVICE ACADEMY RIGHT FOR YOU?   13

    Basic Requirements   14
    Workload   14
    Regimentation   15
    Restricted Social Life   16
    Service Obligation   16
    Desire and Willingness   16
    Self-Assessment   17

3   GETTING READY TO APPLY   21

Start Early   21
Advice for Late Starters   22
Special Situations   23
The "Whole Person" Evaluation Process   23
   Measurement   24
   Point System   24
Shouldering a Heavy Load   25
   Time Management and Study Habits   25
   Balance   26
Academics   26
   Grades and Class Rank   26
   Academic Honors   27
   What Courses Should You Take?   28
   Test Scores   28
   Other Tests   29
Athletics   30
   Varsity Letter   30
   Which Sports?   30
   Team Captain   31
   Awards and Honors   31
Extracurricular Activities   31
   Student Government   32
   Dramatics, Public Speaking, or Debating   32
   Publications   33
   Science, Technology, Engineering, Math (STEM)   33
   Tutoring   34
   Club Leadership   34
   Start Your Own Club   34
Opportunities Outside School   34
   Academy Summer Programs   35
   Boys/Girls State   36
   Scouting/Sea Cadets/Civil Air Patrol   37
   JROTC   37
   Military School   38
Community Service   39
   Schools   39
   Government   39
   Churches and Religious Groups   39
   Charity Work   39
   Environment and Social Services   40

Veterans and Military Support   40
Volunteer Fire/EMS   40
Create Your Own   41
Learning and Adventure   41
Travel   41
Outward Bound–type Programs   41
Summer Programs   42
College Courses/Continuing Education   42
Work   42
Choose Your Own Adventure   42

4   THE APPLICATIONS PROCESS   45

General Tips   46
West Point   47
Preliminary Application   47
Summer Leadership Experience   48
Regional Commanders and Liaison Officers   48
Candidate Portal   49
Candidate Kit Contents   50
Prep School   52
Naval Academy   53
Summer Seminar and Preliminary Application   53
Blue and Gold Officers and Other Admission Staff   54
Candidate Information System   54
Reapplying   55
Coast Guard Academy   55
Merchant Marine Academy   56
Application Process   57
Local Admissions Field Reps   57
Air Force Academy   58
Summer Seminar   58
Academy Liaison Officer   58
Teacher Evaluations and Letters of Recommendation   59
Personal Data Record and Drug and Alcohol Abuse
    Certificate   59
How You Are Evaluated   60
Academics and Class Rank   61
Physical and Sports Leadership   62
Community Influence   62
Recommendations   62
Managing Your Portal   63

5 GETTING A NOMINATION   65

  Understanding Nominations   65
  Sources of Nominations   66
    Senatorial and Congressional Nominations   66
    US Territories and Overseas Possessions   67
    Vice President of the United States   68
    Presidential Nominations   68
      Children of Wounded, Killed, or Missing Veterans   69
      Children of Active Duty or Retired Military   70
      Children of Medal of Honor Winners   70
    Current Military or Reserve Nominations   70
    JROTC/ROTC Honor Units with Distinction   70
    Nominations You Can't Apply For   71
      Service Secretary Nominations for Qualified Alternates   72
      Superintendent's Nominations   72
      Remaining Vacancy Nominations   72
      National Waiting List   72
  International Cadets   73
  Merchant Marine Academy Nominations   73
  Do I Need to Bribe My Congressperson?   74
  How the Congressional Nominations Process Works   76
    Administration   76
    Informational Meeting   77
    Academy Review Board   77
    The Application   78
    Personal Essays   78
    The Interview   79
    Decision   82

6 SPECIAL ISSUES AND CONCERNS   83

  Recruited Athletes   84
    Getting Started   85
    Managing the Process   85
    Physical Qualifications and Health Issues   86
  Economically Disadvantaged/Hardship Candidates   87
  Diversity Recruiting   88
  Women   90
  LGBT   90
  Religious Preference   91
  Foreign/Dual Citizenship   91

Homeschooled or Nontraditional Education   92
Trouble   93
  Drug and Alcohol Use   93
  Encounters with Law Enforcement   93
  Problems in School   94
Former Cadets   94

**7 CANDIDATE FITNESS ASSESSMENT AND
MEDICAL CLEARANCE**   95

Candidate Fitness Assessment   95
  How the CFA Works   96
  Taking the CFA   97
    Preparation   97
    Testing Procedures   98
  The Test   98
    Basketball Throw   98
    Cadence Pull-Ups or Flexed-Arm Hang   99
    Shuttle Run   100
    Modified Sit-Ups (Crunches)   100
    Push-Ups   100
    One-Mile Run   101
    Aftermath   101
  How to Prepare   101
Medical Clearance (DoDMERB)   102
  DoDMERB Outcomes   103
  Preparing for DoDMERB   105
  Height and Weight   106
  Medical Red Flags   106
    Asthma, Seasonal Allergies, Inhaler Use   107
    Learning Disabilities and Other Mental Health Issues   107
    Vision   108
    Surgery, Concussions, and Head Injuries   108
    Medications   109
  Non-Medical Issues   109
    Drug and Alcohol Use   109
    Tattoos, Brands, Piercings, and Body Modifications   109
  The Medical Evaluation Process   110
    The Exam   110
    DoDMERB Web Portal   110
    Evaluation and Decision   111
    Problems after the Examination   112

Waivers and Rebuttals   112
    Timing   113
    Rebuttals   113
    Waivers   114
For More Information   115

8 ACCEPTANCES AND REJECTIONS   117

I Finished My Application. Now What?   117
Candidate Visits   118
Letters of Assurance   118
Types of Admission   119
When Will I Hear?   120
How Will I Hear?   120
What If I Don't Get In?   121
Steps Following Acceptance   122
    Security Clearance   122
    Shoes and Boots   123
    Money Issues   123
    Scholarships   124
    529 Plans   124
    Physical Training   124
    Parents   125
Reporting for Duty   125
    Travel Arrangements   125
    Packing Lists   125
    Reporting In   126
The Shock of Transition and the Morale Curve   126

**APPENDIX I LAWS GOVERNING APPOINTMENTS
TO THE ACADEMIES**   129

United States Military Academy   129
United States Naval Academy   137
United States Air Force Academy   144
United States Coast Guard Academy   152
United States Merchant Marine Academy   154

APPENDIX II   CLASS PROFILES   161

APPENDIX III   RESOURCES   165

    Information about Academic Honor Societies   165
        General Academic Achievement   166
        Specific Academic Areas   166
    Resources about Life at Military Academies   166
    **Resources for Time Management and Studying
        for Students**   167
    **Resources for Writing College Essays and
        Handling Interviews**   167
    Information about Religion at the Academies   168
    **Resources for Preparing for the Candidate
        Fitness Assessment**   168
    Information for Parents   169
    Reporting for Duty   169

APPENDIX IV   PRESIDENTIAL NOMINATION LETTERS   171

    West Point   172
    Naval Academy   173
    Air Force Academy   175

Notes   177

Bibliography   181

Index   183

About the Author   191

Tables

P-1 Timeline for the West Point Application Process, 2014   xix

1-1 Applications and Admissions for the Class of 2018   2

1-2 Which Academy Is Right for You?   12

2-1 Daily Schedule for a Naval Academy Midshipman   15

2-2 Force Field Analysis   19

3-1 What Courses You Should Take in High School   28

3-2 Superscoring   29

3-3 Codes for Submitting Test Scores   29

3-4 High School Activities in Academy Class Profiles   32

3-5 Academy Summer Programs   35

4-1 Application Links   45

5-1 Nominations for US Territories and Overseas Possessions   67

5-2 Nominations Available from All Sources   71

5-3 Potential Interview Questions   81

6-1 Academy Athletic Department Contacts   85

6-2 Diversity Program Websites   89

7-1 Benchmarks for the Candidate Fitness Assessment   96

7-2 CFA Sequence and Timeline   99

7-3 Weight Standards by Service for 68-Inch Height   106

7-4 Tattoo Policies   110

A-1 United States Military Academy Class Profile   162

A-2 United States Naval Academy Class Profile   163

A-3 United States Coast Guard Academy Class Profile   163

A-4 United States Merchant Marine Academy Class Profile   164

A-5 United States Air Force Academy Class Profile   164

Preface

"Dad, can I go to military school?"

My son was in eighth grade when he first decided that he wanted to go into the military. At first, I treated it as I had treated earlier ideas about what he wanted to do when he grew up: be a pastor like his grandfather, go into the theatre (until he found out what apartments in New York City cost), or be a cartoon voice. In each case, I tried to get him information on what it might be like and arranged for him to talk with people. Soon enough, each idea fell by the wayside, which is perfectly normal. I certainly went through my fair share of career ideas.

"Why do you want to go to military school?" I asked. For a lot of kids, military school is a threat: "If you don't straighten up, I'll ship you off to military school!" But he was serious.

"So I can go to West Point and be an Army officer," he said.

I agreed to let him go to a military school for a summer. One way or another, I figured the experience would help him decide if this was a serious option, and indeed, that's what it turned out to be. He liked the discipline and structure, as well as the subject matter and athleticism, and when he came home at the end of that experience, it was pretty clear that he had found his calling.

While my father and brother both served, military service wasn't my personal cup of tea, and I knew very little about it. I understood that the military service academies were very competitive and that you needed a Congressional appointment to be considered, but beyond that the process was new to me. We started to learn about West Point and the academies in general. It turned out that a former boss of mine had actually taught at West Point; we talked with current and former officers who'd been to the Academy and people who went the Reserve Officers' Training Corps (ROTC) route instead.

Applying to a military academy turned out to be the equivalent of applying to three or four civilian schools. There was the regular application process, the Congressional nomination process, medical and physical reviews, and much more.

At West Point alone, over fifteen thousand candidates (over sixty thousand for all academies combined) start the applications process. Less than a third of them finish it. Some figure out that they aren't going to be competitive, some get derailed with specific problems, and some get lost and drop out even though they might have gotten in.

In addition to the usual stuff like grades and SATs, you have to get nominated by your congressperson or senator. (There are a few exceptions.) For my son, that meant filling out three questionnaires, each containing multiple essay questions, then going before a board of military officers and civilians who recommended the people who would—and would not—receive a nomination.

A nomination alone doesn't get you in. There's a regular applications process as well, where you add references and transcripts and SAT scores and information about your extracurricular activities.

You have to pass a fitness assessment and a medical exam. Even if you're a good athlete, you'd better practice. The medical examiners (called DoDMERB) demand extensive evidence that you're fit and healthy. Disqualifications happen, but fortunately there's also a waiver process.

You're not completely alone; there's a local representative for each academy for each region who'll answer your emails. Most members of Congress hold information meetings for students and parents considering going after a nomination. For the most part, however, it's up to you and your family—and it's often a team effort.

Table P-1 shows the official timeline of activities for the year my son applied to West Point.

We had a thousand questions along the way: What's Boys State? (Boys State is a summer program. Doing well there is surprisingly valuable.) Can he get into the Summer Leadership Experience? (No, but he did get accepted anyway.) How tough is the Candidate Fitness Assessment? (It's pretty tough; practice a lot.) And so on. We asked everyone we could find who'd been through the process or who'd gone to a service academy. I prowled discussion boards and forums wherever I could find them.

Because he wanted to go to West Point, he knew he had to make outstanding grades, get a varsity letter in sports, and demonstrate leadership. Whether he got in or not, I could see that the act of trying all by itself was making him a better, stronger person. He joined our local volunteer fire department and became a qualified firefighter/EMT. By his senior year, he commanded an ambulance.

Table P-1. Timeline for the West Point Application Process, 2014

U. S. Military Academy Candidate Timeline, 2014 (for Class of 2018)

This time line is provided as an UNOFFICIAL and APPROXIMATE aid for applying to the U. S. Military Academy at West Point. Please check official USMA publications for the most accurate information and dates.

Event	Timing / Notes
Take at least 1 SAT, ACT, or PSAT by the fall of junior year. Save your score reports.	
SAT/ACT Testing (must take writing portion)	Test multiple times and send ALL scores in. SAT code 2934, ACT code 2976. Final ACT, final SAT (Dec/Jan)
Candidate Questionnaire and SLS Application Open	THE SOONER THE BETTER
Complete Candidate Questionnaire (CQ)	PSAT, SAT, or ACT needed.
Apply for Summer Leadership Seminar (SLS)	(1st two weeks of June)
Apply to Boys/Girls State (recommended)	www.boysandgirlsstate.org (1 boy, 1 girl session)
Contact Field Force Representative	See the "liaisons" tab of your candidate portal for POC.
Train for Candidate Fitness Assessment (CFA)	Download "CFA instructions" from portal
Apply for Nomination	SOONER=BETTER. (See the "Nominations" tab of your portal.)
Complete Nominations Application	Most deadlines are in SEP or OCT. Don't be late!
Prep your 3 School Officials (1 math, 1 English, 1 Physics or Chemistry)	Send the SOE form through portal—ensure they know it is coming. Select and inform.
Arrange with your school to get your 6-semester transcript at the end of the year.	As early as possible.
USMA Application Process Opens June/July	
Complete Application for Admissions	THE SOONER THE BETTER! Only fully qualified applicants will be considered.
Complete the academic items on your application first (official transcript, class rank, ACT/SAT)	Complete ASAP
Conditional Offers (Letter of Assurance) go out: LOA=fully qualified+nomination=OFFER!	If you qualify, USMA will contact you.
Complete Candidate Fitness Assessment (CFA) early, especially if you are in a fall sport	Prepare and Practice—don't put this off!
Take Medical Exam. If you don't get mail from DoDMERB within a couple wks, call your FF rep!	YOU schedule exams through DoDMERB
Field Force Interviews	Check the "liaisons" tab of your portal
Apply to at least two other colleges—one you may get into and one you're sure you'll get into	You need to have other options.
Apply for an Army ROTC scholarship at www.goarmy.com/rotc. Both West Point & ROTC make officers!	Scholarship boards meet in OCT, JAN and MAR
Complete follow-up on medical issues—monitor status on DODMETS website.	Complete Remedials quickly—use DoDMETS website
Ensure application is complete (all "green" + transcripts on candidate portal)	USMA accepts verified score and activity updates
Nomination interviews	Prepare by researching
Nomination notifications (nomination does NOT necessarily=offer of admission, but is a prerequisite...no nom=no offer.	Required!
Submit fall transcript before 28 FEB. Look for "7 semesters received" on portal.	Required!
College students submit fall transcript as soon as ready, plus two college School Official Evaluations	Incomplete files close 1 MAR
USMA Application Process Closes Feb 26	
Admissions Committee meets	
Majority of Offers of Admission made (USMA no longer conducts "rolling" admissions)	15 April deadline
New Class Enters — late June/early July	

Month headings (Junior Year then Senior Year): Dec | Jan | Feb | Mar | Apr | May | Jun | Jul | Aug | Sep | Oct | Nov | Dec | Jan | Feb | Mar | Apr | May | Jun | Jul

WHAT DOES AN ARMY OFFICER DO? Find out at GoArmy.com/officer

ONLINE APPLICATION FOUND AT: http://www.usma.edu/admissions/SitePages/Apply.aspx

While he necessarily did most of the work on his various applications, it turned out that applying was a family affair. From the spring of his junior year until he received his Big Fat Envelope (BFE) from West Point signifying he'd been admitted to the Class of 2018, we all had work to do. And once he was accepted, it turned out there was still a whole lot that had to be done.

In July 2014, we drove him to West Point for "R-Day," when new cadets report for basic training, known as "Beast Barracks." It was a long, rewarding, and ultimately happy journey. For the right young man or young woman, a military academy education is an amazing opportunity. It comes at a price—not so much in dollars, but in extremely challenging work, and a service obligation following graduation. If it's the place for you, however, that price is well worth it.

We were fortunate to get advice and help from many people along the way, but we often wished there was a book that would lay out the process and give us the necessary guidance. Because I'd written a number of career and business books (and a few novels), and had worked with the federal government and the US defense establishment as a trainer and coach, I decided to write it myself.

My thanks and gratitude go to numerous people who helped with the process and with this book, and I apologize if I've inadvertently left anyone out.

In particular, I thank my hardworking agent, Maryann Karinch of the Rudy Agency; Major General Guy Bourne, USA (Ret.); Ted Leemann; LTC Michael A. Lockwood; Col. Deborah McDonald; Col. Michael C. Dougherty; Gene McIntyre; Cadet Lauren Cooper; Major Daniel Weiss; Francis DeMaro; Ryan Yanoshak; MSG Dean Welch; Lt. Matthew Stroup; TSGT Todd Kabalan; Debra Dalton; Rocky and Cindy Mengle; Connie English; Elise Brown Hughes; Jim McCormick; and Joe Wiedemann. My thanks as well to my wife, Deborah Singer Dobson, who suggested I write this book, and to my son James Dobson, for letting me use him as a case study.

How to Use This Book

This book describes the step-by-step process for applying to and being accepted by a military service academy. Some parts of the process are fairly mechanical in nature: no matter what school you apply to, you'll have to provide certain standard information. Other parts are more individual, such as figuring out how to show the special accomplishments and characteristics that make you stand out. There are some potential obstacles you may face, such as obtaining medical clearance or resolving dual citizenship issues.

Every year sees some changes in the process. The calendar and timeline is definitely different. The economy and the military state of the world changes, which influences the number of applicants and sometimes the number of students admitted. New technology comes along that affects the process.

Rather that produce an entirely new edition of this book every year, we offer a free downloadable PDF with the current year's calendar and timeline, any known changes to the process, and any corrections we may need to make to the information contained in this book. Please visit http://militaryacademy.info for your copy. You can also sign up to receive occasional emails during the application cycle with the latest news, and there's a forum where you can ask any questions or share experiences.

The process of applying to a military service academy is stressful, lengthy, and difficult. However, the potential rewards can be life changing. We hope you'll find this guide a useful and practical tool in navigating the process, and wish you the very best of luck.

—Michael Dobson

❶

About the Academies

Many nations around the world operate military service academies to train future officers for their armed forces. The United States operates five service academies: four are military. In order of their founding, they are the United States Military Academy (better known as West Point), the United States Naval Academy (which serves both the US Navy and the US Marine Corps), the United States Coast Guard Academy, and the United States Air Force Academy. Students are considered to be on active military duty for their entire time at the academy and become commissioned officers (2nd lieutenants or ensigns) upon graduation.

The fifth is the United States Merchant Marine Academy. It was established to train officers to serve on US-flagged merchant marine vessels. Graduates of the Merchant Marine Academy can also choose to work in certain other maritime industry roles or take an active duty appointment in any of the military services.

The academies are tuition free—students even receive a small salary, which pays for books, certain uniform items, and incidental expenses. (The Merchant Marine Academy is a little different.) Graduates have a service obligation following graduation, usually five years of active duty. Typically, a graduate serves in the same branch as the academy, but it's possible for a graduate of one academy to seek commissioning in another service.

Service academies normally are ranked among the best colleges in the country. In 2015, *U.S. News and World Report*'s college rankings of public liberal arts colleges nationwide listed the Naval Academy, West Point, and the Air Force Academy as #1, #2, and #3 respectively.[1]

Class sizes are small, educational options are extensive, and the experiences offered students are many and varied. Cadets and midshipmen often study around the world, attend advanced military training, and shadow units in the field.

So if you go to one of the service academies, you get (a) free tuition, (b) a salary, (c) a world-class education, (d) unparalleled experiences, (e) and a guaranteed job upon graduation. Pretty sweet, right?

On the other hand, academy life is far more regimented and restricted than anything you'll encounter at a civilian college or university. The school year is longer—July through May—and you can't just go away for the weekend whenever you please. The workload can be daunting, physical and military training is mandatory, and the discipline is strict. It's not for everybody. While some people thrive and grow, others quickly discover that this is not the life that suits them.

If you have an ambition to serve your country as an officer and leader, and are willing to accept the extra constraints and pressure, an academy education can change your life.

Of course, admission is highly competitive. Table 1-1 shows the numbers for the Class of 2018 at each academy.

Table I-I.   Applications and Admissions for the Class of 2018

Academy	Applied	Admitted	Percent
USMA (West Point)	13827	1257	9%
USNA (Navy)	17618	1191	7%
USCGA (Coast Guard)	4000	240	6%
USMMA (Merchant Marine)	2217	252	11%
USAFA (Air Force)	9706	1190	12%
TOTALS	47368	4130	9%

While those numbers may look pretty daunting, the situation is better than it looks. For one thing, a large number of candidates never complete their applications, some because they realize their interests lie elsewhere, and some because they realize early in the process that they won't be competitive.

For the US Merchant Marine Academy Class of 2018, for example, out of 2,217 applications, 1,272 weren't completed—a rate of nearly 60 percent! (The other schools don't publish this information, but I've been told the incomplete application rate is pretty consistent.) Of the 945 candidates who completed their applications, 688 (about 70 percent) met all of the criteria. A little more than half of those (378) were offered appointments, resulting in the final reporting-in class of 252. If you're serious about going to a service academy and work hard to prepare yourself, your personal chances of success are a lot higher than you might think.

Let's take a closer look at each of the five service academies. To avoid taking sides in school rivalries, I've listed them in the order of their founding.

- United States Military Academy (USMA or West Point), founded 1802
- United States Naval Academy (USNA), founded 1845
- United States Coast Guard Academy (USCGA), founded 1876
- United States Merchant Marine Academy (USMMA), founded 1943
- United States Air Force Academy (USAFA), founded 1954

UNITED STATES MILITARY ACADEMY (WEST POINT)

The oldest of the military service academies is the United States Military Academy (West Point or USMA), located about fifty miles north of New York City on the western bank of the Hudson River, next to the town of Highland Falls. The entire West Point military reservation covers nearly sixteen thousand acres, including a military community and the training facility known as Camp Buckner. Cadets live and study for the most part in the central campus area. West Point is a National Historic Landmark and a popular tourist destination.

West Point is also the oldest continuously-operating Army post in the United States, originally established during the American Revolutionary War for the purpose of keeping British Royal Navy ships from sailing up the Hudson River and dividing the Thirteen Colonies. The Polish military engineer Tadeusz Kościuszko designed and oversaw construction of the fortifications at a narrow S-bend on the Hudson beginning in 1778. In 1780, its commander Benedict Arnold tried unsuccessfully to sell the post to the British.

In March 1802, an act of Congress established the United States Military Academy at West Point. Originally, there were few standards for either admission or length of study; it graduated its first officer in October 1802. Early cadets ranged in age from ten to thirty-seven, but by the War of 1812, West Point began to standardize and develop itself as an education institution.

The United States Military Academy takes its educational philosophy and direction from its sixth superintendent, Sylvanus Thayer, often called the "father of West Point." Under Thayer's leadership,

West Point became the first engineering school in the United States. In the early years of the twentieth century, Douglas MacArthur instituted the first Cadet Honor Committee, added a new emphasis on history and humanities, and pushed for an end to hazing of plebes, as freshmen at West Point are known.

By the time of the American Civil War, nearly every general officer on both the Union and Confederate sides was a graduate of West Point, a tradition that has continued. Although a number of important Army leaders didn't go to West Point (General Colin Powell, for example), the percentage of general officers who are West Point graduates remains very high. West Point leaders have made a difference in many aspects of American life and history. West Point–trained engineers designed and built the majority of the railway lines, bridges, and roads that formed the basis for our nation's growth in the nineteenth century.

The "Long Gray Line," as West Point cadets are called, has produced many notable Americans:

- Buzz Aldrin, astronaut
- Frank Borman, astronaut and airline CEO
- Michael Collins, astronaut
- George Armstrong Custer, general
- Dwight D. Eisenhower, general and president of the United States
- Leslie Groves, general and head of the Manhattan Project
- Robert E. Lee, general
- Douglas MacArthur, general
- George Patton, general

There are even some notable figures who attended West Point but didn't graduate, including Edgar Allen Poe, James McNeill Whistler, and Timothy Leary.

West Point was accredited in 1925, and began awarding bachelor of science degrees to graduates beginning in 1933. (Even today, regardless of academic major, all West Point graduates hold a bachelor of science degree because of the strong engineering background required of all cadets.) West Point was an early adopter of computers, and in 2006 was named one of Americas "most wired" campuses.

UNITED STATES NAVAL ACADEMY

The United States Naval Academy (Naval Academy or USNA), established in 1845, is located in Annapolis, Maryland, a little over thirty miles from the nation's capital. The 338-acre campus was built on the grounds of the former Fort Severn. Like West Point, the Naval Academy is a National Historic Landmark.

The mission of the Naval Academy is to train officers for the US Navy and the US Marine Corps, and graduates are commissioned as ensigns (Navy) or 2nd lieutenants (Marine Corps). The service commitment of a graduate is five years, except for certain professions like pilot.

Originally, midshipmen would complete an eight-month course at the Philadelphia Naval School, but the bulk of their naval education came at sea. In 1842, midshipmen allegedly plotted to commit mutiny so they could turn their training ship, the USS *Somers*, into a pirate vessel. The captain had three men hanged, including a midshipman whose father happened to be the secretary of war. That, combined with Commodore Matthew Perry's desire to modernize the Navy, led to the new school. Perry himself helped establish the curriculum, a five-year program in which students spent two years at sea. Today, midshipmen complete three cruises as part of their training, although some serve in aviation squadrons or Marine Corps units, not necessarily all at sea.

During the American Civil War, the Naval Academy was temporarily relocated to Rhode Island and was substantially rebuilt and expanded in the aftermath of the war. In 1933, the Naval Academy began awarding bachelor of science degrees.

Notable Naval Academy alumni include the following:

- Richard E. Byrd, arctic explorer
- Jimmy Carter, president of the United States
- William Halsey, Jr., admiral
- Robert A. Heinlein, science fiction writer
- Jim Lovell, astronaut
- John McCain, US senator and presidential nominee
- Albert A. Michelson, physicist and Nobel Prize winner
- Chester Nimitz, admiral
- Ross Perot, business executive and presidential candidate
- Walter Schirra, astronaut
- Alan Shepard, astronaut
- Roger Staubach, football player
- Montel Williams, television host

UNITED STATES COAST GUARD ACADEMY

The United States Coast Guard Academy (USCGA), the smallest of the five, is located on the banks of the Thames River in New London,

Connecticut. Each year, the Coast Guard Academy admits only 250 students, of whom an average of two hundred graduate.

The USCGA was originally called the School of Instruction of the Revenue Cutter Service (the Revenue Cutter Service was one of the predecessors of the modern Coast Guard), located in Massachusetts and later in Maryland. In 1910, the school moved to its current home on the site of the Revolutionary War–era Fort Trumbull. Because of its long heritage, the Coast Guard Academy is listed on the National Register of Historic Places.

When the Revenue Cutter Service merged with the US Life-Saving Service in 1915, the School of Instruction became the United States Coast Guard Academy.

Because of the school's seagoing mission, the USCGA has operated a series of training ships, from the schooner USRC *Dobbin* to the current USCGC *Eagle*. The *Eagle* is the only active commissioned sailing vessel in US service; it was originally taken by the United States as war reparations from Germany following World War II, where it had also been a training ship.

There's one major difference between the Coast Guard Academy and all the other service academies: you don't need a Congressional nomination to get in. (The School of Instruction's first superintendent, Captain John Henriques, upset at the poor quality of political appointees in the Revenue Cutter Service bureaucracy, strenuously objected to the idea of nominations, and finally prevailed.)

SPECIAL NOTE! The United States Coast Guard Academy is the only one of the service academies that doesn't require a Congressional nomination.

Because the mission of the Coast Guard Academy is tightly focused, the school offers only eight majors, with government and management the only two majors that are not STEM (Science, Technology, Engineering, Mathematics) topics.

You'll often see the Coast Guard Academy at the top of the lists of hardest schools to get into. Although fewer people apply to the Coast Guard Academy than to either West Point or the Naval Academy, the small class size means that an even lower percentage of applicants get in.

Should you apply? If the Coast Guard and sea service is your passion, absolutely. If you're looking for a more general education and your long-term goals lie elsewhere, the Coast Guard Academy may not be the place for you.

Notable alumni of the Coast Guard Academy include G. William Miller, former chairman of the Federal Reserve and secretary of the Treasury; Admiral Thad Allen, who led the response to the Deepwater Horizon oil spill along the Gulf Coast; and aviator Elmer Stone, pilot on the first transatlantic flight.

UNITED STATES MERCHANT MARINE ACADEMY

The Merchant Marine isn't actually a military service, so the United States Merchant Marine Academy (USMMA) is a service academy, as distinct from a military service academy, even though its students are called midshipmen and they often go into officer roles on the fleet of US-flagged merchant vessels. (Midshipmen are, however, part of the US Navy Reserve.)

SPECIAL NOTE! Because the United States Merchant Marine Academy serves the private sector, midshipmen are not considered members of the US military and therefore don't receive the salary that cadets and midshipmen at the other academies get, except for time spent at sea on merchant vessels. While the US government still pays for tuition, uniforms, room and board, and even some medical expenses, cadets are responsible for personal items and incidental expenses. For the Class of 2017, first-year mandatory fees totaled $2,905, most of which went toward a laptop; $765 for the next two classes; and $1,380 for midshipmen in their final year.

If you own or operate a US civilian–owned merchant vessel for commerce in and out of the navigable waters of the United States, you're part of the Merchant Marine. (Some of these ships are chartered by the US government and operated by the Military Sealift Command.)

So why does the US government have an academy to train officers for private industry ships? There are many reasons from safety to economic development, but one important reason is national security. In times of war, the US Merchant Marine can be turned into a Navy auxiliary. In World War II, the United States operated the Lend-Lease program; merchant mariners braved U-boats and other menaces to transport vitally important cargo to American allies.

The US Merchant Marine Academy was established at Kings Point, New York (about twenty miles east of New York City), in 1943.

Its campus is listed on the National Register of Historic Places. (The US Merchant Marine Corps of Cadets is slightly older, having started in 1938 before the Academy got a permanent home.) Its immediate goal was to meet the demand for qualified merchant marine operators, and it graduated nearly seven thousand merchant marine officers before the end of the war in 1945.

While not being a military service, USMMA midshipmen have served in every major US combat action since World War II, and over 140 have given their lives. As a result, the USMMA Corps of Cadets is the only service academy privileged to carry a regimental battle standard.

Initial Academy training was narrowly focused because of the need to turn out officers in a hurry, but by 1948, the US Merchant Marine Academy's curriculum was a regular four-year college program similar to the other service academies. Like the USNA and USCGA, part of the Merchant Marine Academy training is conducted at sea, currently in the T/V *Kings Pointer*, a former NASA rocket recovery vessel.

Like the Coast Guard Academy, the Merchant Marine Academy offers bachelor of science degrees in a limited range of majors: marine transportation, logistics, marine engineering, and shipyard management, among others. Graduates are expected to be able to qualify for a license as either a Third Mate or Third Assistant Engineer, unlimited tonnage, upon oceans, and during their time at the academy, spend a minimum of three hundred days as a crew member aboard an American merchant vessel.

SPECIAL NOTE! The United States Merchant Marine Academy offers graduates the widest range of ways to fulfill service requirements.

Because of the unusual nature of the Merchant Marine Academy, its graduates have the widest range of options to fulfill their five-year minimum service obligation. They can go to sea as licensed officers on any US-flagged merchant ships; they can choose to apply for an active duty commission in any branch of the US military; or they can hold a variety of civilian jobs in the maritime industry—often at very good salaries.

Many Merchant Marine graduates refer to the Academy as "one of the nation's best kept secrets." Although the program is as intensive and demanding as in any of the other academies, the fact that it is less well known means there's a bit less competition for each slot. While some applicants, especially those with a primary interest in the Naval

Academy, consider the Merchant Marine Academy as a back-up plan, you might decide after a closer look that it's your top choice after all.

Notable alumni of the Merchant Marine Academy include automation pioneer John Diebold, Nobel Prize–winning physicists Henry Kendall and Martin Perl, and *All in the Family* star Carroll O'Connor.

UNITED STATES AIR FORCE ACADEMY

The United States Air Force only became a separate military service in 1947; previously it was part of the US Army. In the same way that Marine Corps officer candidates attend the Naval Academy, would-be Army Air Force officers attended West Point. It became increasingly clear, however, that the training needs of future Air Force officers were different enough that the new service needed its own academy.

The United States Air Force Academy officially came into being in 1954, but its permanent campus in Colorado Springs, Colorado, wasn't ready until 1958. The campus, famous for its modernist style, covers 18,500 acres along the east edge of the Rampart Range of the Rocky Mountains. It was designated a National Historic Landmark in 2004, and is one of the biggest tourist attractions in the state.

Like its cousins at West Point and Annapolis, the Air Force Academy offers a wide range of majors. It's also a major research institution, the highest of all undergraduate-only universities in federally funded research.

Because the Air Force Academy is the newest of the service academies, its list of notable alumni is smaller. Nevertheless, in its short existence it has produced 39 astronauts, 35 Rhodes Scholars, and 403 generals.

UNITED STATES SENIOR MILITARY COLLEGES/ROTC

Besides the service academies, there are other routes to consider if your goal is to become a military officer. Many colleges and universities offer Reserve Officer Training Corps (ROTC) programs, and scholarships are often available for those programs. While there are some traditional benefits associated with a service academy degree, people that come through the ROTC program can do just as well—General Colin Powell, for example, took ROTC at City College of New York, and rose to become National Security Advisor, chairman of the Joint Chiefs of Staff, and secretary of state.

There are six ROTC schools classified as Senior Military Colleges (SMC). Their ROTC programs are patterned after the federal service academies, with a corps of cadets operating in a military environment. Those six schools are as follows:

- Norwich University, Vermont
- Texas A&M University
- The Citadel, South Carolina
- University of North Georgia
- Virginia Military Institute
- Virginia Polytechnic Institute and State University (Virginia Tech)

PREPARATORY SCHOOLS

If you're not quite qualified but the potential is there, you may be considered for admission to the preparatory school associated with the academy you've applied to. You can't apply to the preparatory schools directly, however. Like the service academies, tuition is free and cadet candidates receive a small stipend.

The preparatory school program is one academic year in length, and during that time, cadet candidates reapply to their academies for the following year. Most prep school students receive appointments, but not all. If you don't get in, or are offered an appointment but choose not to accept it, you can return to civilian life without penalty, or if you're currently a service enlisted person, return to your previous role. The three large academies operate their own prep schools; the two smaller academies send students elsewhere. The schools and their locations are listed below:

- West Point: United States Military Academy Preparatory School, West Point, New York
- Naval Academy: Naval Academy Preparatory School, Newport, Rhode Island
- Air Force Academy: United States Air Force Academy Preparatory School, Colorado Springs, Colorado
- Coast Guard Academy: Either Georgia Military College or the Marion (Alabama) Military Institute
- Merchant Marine Academy: New Mexico Military Institute

GRADUATE SCHOOLS

While the service academies are undergraduate only, awarding no degree beyond a bachelor of science, there are many opportunities for post-graduate education. If you pursue a military career, you're expected to hold a post-graduate degree before you're promoted to lieutenant colonel or commander, but many military officers do this earlier in their careers, some immediately upon graduation. This additional education is at government expense, but you incur an additional service obligation in exchange.

The US government runs a number of higher educational institutions itself, aimed at the specialized needs of the military. Medical professionals may attend the Uniformed Services University of the Health Sciences; other schools include the National Defense Intelligence College, the US Army Command and General Staff College, the Naval Postgraduate School, and the Air Force Institute of Technology.

WHICH ACADEMY SHOULD YOU CHOOSE?

As we mentioned earlier, the tremendous benefits of an academy education come with obligations and costs. For some people, it's the perfect environment—for others, not so much. In the next chapter, we'll explore whether a service academy is the right choice for you, but before we leave this chapter, there's one more important question: if you're going to an academy, which one?

When our family started the process, one piece of advice we were given is that it was smart to apply to all the academies, not just one. There are pros and cons to this approach. On the good side, your chances of getting a nomination or admission are greater; on the bad side, people may question your commitment to a given service, which won't help. Our advice (supported by interviews with academy admissions professionals) is that you should do what's right for you.

If you're interested in multiple services, by all means apply to different academies. If your interests are more narrowly focused, put your energy where you most want to be. In certain cases, a single interest can make it worthwhile for you to consider more than one academy. If you want to be a pilot, for example, both the Air Force and the Navy have great opportunities—and it will be easy to explain why you're applying to both academies.

If you apply to multiple academies, expect to be asked what your real priorities are, and which academy you prefer. (Some Congressional nomination applications require you to rate the academies to which you are applying in the order of preference.) All the academies (as well as the Congressional nominators) are interested in commitment and desire along with the general criteria like grades and athletic ability.

That being said, even if you have an interest in a particular branch of service, you can often choose to serve in that branch even if you went to another academy (a few people each year do this), and you may find that the other service is more to your liking than you'd expect. Fleet Admiral Chester Nimitz, commander-in-chief of the Pacific Ocean Areas during World War II, wanted to go to West Point to become an Army officer, but there were no appointments available. There was one Naval Academy appointment available, so he pursued that instead, and went on to a very distinguished career indeed.

Table 1-2 lists some goals along with the academies that might be most suitable for you in pursuing them.

If your goal isn't listed, write it down and research how well each academy will meet your needs. Then plan to apply to each one that will help you achieve your goals.

Table 1-2. Which Academy Is Right for You?

Goal	West Point	Naval Academy	Coast Guard Academy	Merchant Marine Academy	Air Force Academy
Attorney/JAG	X	X			X
Aviation		X	X		X
Civilian Job				X	
Command Fighting Troops	X	X (Marine Corps)			
Engineering/STEM	X	X	X	X	X
Free Education	X	X	X		X
Med School[2]	X	X		X	X
Sea Service		X	X	X	

[2]Generally, the academies aren't there to prepare future physicians; there are other routes to pursue if you want a free education in exchange for a service obligation. That being said, up to 2–3% of the graduating classes of West Point, Naval Academy, and Air Force Academy are eligible to go directly to med school following graduation.

2

Is a Service Academy
Right for You?

The advantages of going to a service academy are many, but it's not exactly a "free" education even though there's no tuition. Cadets and midshipmen carry a heavy workload; they live in a highly regimented environment; they have little opportunity to party; and even after they graduate, they still have a minimum of five more years in the same sort of environment.

For some potential applicants, the discussion ends right here. If this isn't the place for you, you should probably direct your focus elsewhere. Others, however, grow and prosper in this environment—but everybody has bad days.

If you're not 100 percent sure a service academy is the right environment for you, that's okay. Some doubt is normal, and you may still have some qualms about your choice even on the day you report for duty. If you go to an academy, we guarantee that there will be days when you deeply regret your decision and think seriously about leaving. That, too, is perfectly normal.

SPECIAL NOTE! For the first two years at an academy, you can walk away at any time with no obligation. (If you came to an academy from the enlisted ranks, you return to finish your military service obligation.) When you report for your third year, you are expected to recommit to your service obligation, and from that point on, if you fail to graduate you may be required to repay the cost of your education and/or complete your service obligation in the enlisted ranks, though this penalty isn't always imposed.

When my son visited West Point for his overnight stay (see chapter 8), the cadet he was rooming with told him, "West Point is really cool before you come here. West Point is really cool after you leave.

West Point is really cool if you're an outsider. But when you're here, West Point is definitely not cool." The same, we're sure, can be said of all academies.

In spite of these potential downsides, a lot of students clearly think the experience is overall worthwhile. The vast majority of cadets and midshipmen go on to graduate: over 80 percent in most cases. For all colleges and universities, the six-year graduation rate is about 60 percent. (The Merchant Marine Academy's graduation rate is closer to the national average.)

BASIC REQUIREMENTS

Every candidate must meet the following general qualifications:

- Be at least seventeen years of age but have not reached your twenty-third birthday by July 1 of the year you enter the academy
- Be a citizen of the United States of America (there are certain exceptions for authorized international students)
- Be unmarried, not pregnant, and not legally responsible for the support of any children
- Be in good physical and mental health
- Be physically fit

These requirements are absolute. If you do not meet all of them, you can't be considered for admission. (The Coast Guard Academy also requires that you be debt-free.)

As we've discussed, you also need great grades, top test scores, and athletic achievement. In those areas, you're ranked against the others who apply. Appendix II provides class profiles of the incoming classes for each academy. You can benchmark yourself against those profiles to see where you're strong, and where you could be stronger. Don't worry if you are below average in some areas. While academies want well-rounded candidates, nobody is equally strong at everything.

WORKLOAD

Table 2-1 provides an example of a daily schedule for a midshipman at the US Naval Academy:

Table 2-1. Daily Schedule for a Naval Academy Midshipman

5:30 a.m.	Arise for personal fitness workout (optional)
6:30 a.m.	Reveille (all hands out of bed)
6:30–7:00 a.m.	Special instruction period for plebes
7:00 a.m.	Morning meal formation
7:15 a.m.	Morning meal
7:55–11:45 a.m.	Four class periods, 50 minutes each
12:05 p.m.	Noon meal formation
12:10 p.m.	Noon meal
12:50–1:20 p.m.	Company training time
1:30–3:30 p.m.	Fifth and sixth class periods
3:45–6:00 p.m.	Varsity and intramural athletics, extracurricular and personal activities; drill and parades twice weekly in the fall and spring
6:30–7:15 p.m.	Evening Meal
8:00–11:00 p.m.	Study period
Midnight	Taps for all midshipmen

Of course, that's just the basic day. In addition to all of this, there are military duties, preparation for inspections, extra academic instruction if necessary, clubs, and a social life—when you can fit it in. Participating in sports is mandatory. The minimum daily practice requirement can be just the beginning for athletes in varsity sports.

Notice that there are six class periods. At most colleges, fifteen semester hours is a full-time schedule. At the academies, anywhere from eighteen to twenty-one semester hours is a more typical course load.

REGIMENTATION

At a service academy, you're in the military. (Even though that's technically not true for the Merchant Marine Academy, it still follows the same model as the others.) You wear a uniform each day, you salute your superior officers, you follow orders, and you keep your barracks (dorm) room ready for inspection.

The West Point catalog quotes a cadet: "The Army has a place for everything and a way to fold everything. In our closet, clothes have to be hung in a certain order. Our underwear has to be folded 'just so' and placed in a certain part of the drawer. The inside of our desk must be neat and our books stacked on the shelf from the tallest to the shortest. In the medicine cabinet, the razor has to be on a particular shelf and turned a certain way. We have to dust, sweep, clean the sinks, and make sure the mirrors are clean."

While hazing as such has been abolished at the academies, plebes (freshmen) in particular are still subject to a variety of customs and rituals. They are expected to memorize a great deal of academy tradition and recite it on command. During plebe summer at the Naval Academy, plebes are expected to memorize and recite on command the location of the next formation, the uniform required, the day's menu, and other information.

Messing up will earn you demerits, for which marching is a typical penalty. At West Point, it's called "walking the yard," and a cadet who accumulates one hundred hours or more of marching penalty is known as a "century man."

RESTRICTED SOCIAL LIFE

You won't find any of the service academies on the list of great party schools, so if that's the college experience you want, you should probably look elsewhere.

You need a pass in order to leave campus, and especially as an underclassman, the number of passes you can earn is limited. You won't have a car until you're an upperclassman (usually a junior). After taps, you're generally expected to be in your room. Cadets and midshipmen can date each other, except that plebes can't date upperclassmen. Many people date outside the academies, but that carries its own challenges.

SERVICE OBLIGATION

For your first two years at an academy, you can drop out without being obligated to serve in the military (except if you were already in the military when you enrolled). When you start your junior year, they'll readminister your oath, and now it's for real. If you leave now, you can end up serving your time in the enlisted ranks or in some cases having to repay the government the cost of your education.

The minimum service commitment is five years, but if you elect to go to graduate school or flight school or any of the more demanding and expensive options, you'll take on an Additional Duty Service Obligation (ADSO). Graduate school carries a three-year ADSO; medical school costs ten years.

DESIRE AND WILLINGNESS

Shortly after my son started his application file at West Point, we arranged a visit with the local West Point representative. (See chapter 4 for how to arrange this.)

While most of the interview involved my son, he had a question for me as well: had I attended an academy or been in the military myself. "It's important that this be your son's choice, not yours," he told me, and went on to tell the story of a West Point student who had committed suicide. He left behind his class ring along with a note for his father that read, "You wanted this more than I did."

This is not to make you worried about suicide. Sadly, suicides among young people are all too common, and happen at all universities. The lesson was about the wrong kind of parental pressure.

Although students can leave an academy if it's not a good fit, the fear of disappointing parents and loved ones can be a huge burden on someone who gets into one and who truly doesn't want to be there. This can be extra troublesome for someone who comes from a long tradition of military service.

As far as family pressures are concerned, you can do worse than to follow the example of Gen. Douglas MacArthur. MacArthur's son visited West Point with his father. Both of them realized almost immediately that it was the wrong place for young Arthur. General MacArthur is known for his utter devotion to West Point, but he didn't push his son to attend.

And if it turns out that you leave the academy, no matter what the reason, take to heart the words of a former military academy instructor who told a parents group meeting, "Make sure that your cadet or midshipmen knows that if they have the merit to get into an academy, they also have the merit to succeed no matter what their ultimate direction in life."

> **SPECIAL NOTE!** Attend (or don't attend) a service academy for *your* reasons. If one of them is to please your parents or other people, that's okay—as long as that's not the *only* reason.

SELF-ASSESSMENT

You may be 100 percent certain that an academy is the right place for you, and that's great. You can skip this section if you like. If you've got some doubt about whether you should pursue this option, that's okay, too. Here are some ideas to help you.

Only you can make the ultimate decision about whether a service academy education is right for you, but you don't have to make it alone. Talk to current and former military officers about life in the service. See if you can find people who attended a service academy who will share their experience. Read about life at the academies (see the suggested reading list). Talk to family members, other trusted adults, and peers.

As we said, doubt (and a little fear) are normal. You'll learn more as you move forward through the process, and that will help.

Here are some specific questions to ponder. Don't stop with our lists of options and issues; add your own as appropriate.

Why do you want to go to a service academy? Some motives are about service, and others are more pragmatic or financial. You'll probably find a number of answers.

- Desire to serve your country
- Desire to be a military (or merchant marine) officer
- Interest in special training (pilot, doctor, nuclear engineer) or job experience
- Like to work in a highly disciplined and structured environment
- Desire to be part of a tradition
- Family history or family motives
- Low-cost, high-quality education
- Guaranteed employment upon graduation
- Being part of a powerful alumni network

What do you fear most about going to a service academy? There will be things about your academy experience you don't like, and every cadet and midshipman, as we've noted, thinks about quitting at least once. Make sure you look carefully at the downsides as part of making your decision.

- Being mistreated during plebe year
- Not being able to get away and unwind when I want to
- The regimentation, from prescribed uniforms to the organization of your closet
- Not being able to see boyfriend/girlfriend
- Not sure I can handle the workload
- Fear of failure, of disappointing parents or other people
- Don't really want to serve in the military after graduation

What are your alternatives if you don't go to a military academy? Always compare a potential choice against the potential alternatives. If you're competitive for a service academy, you're definitely competitive for many other top schools. If you don't go to an academy but still seek military service, you have options ranging from enlistment to ROTC to Officer Candidate School (OCS). If you need a free or low-cost education, there are other scholarship opportunities. If you want to be a pilot, a doctor, or a lawyer, there are routes that don't involve the military. How attractive are these options? What are the pros and cons of your alternate choices?

- Seek an ROTC scholarship
- Take ROTC without seeking a scholarship
- Seek a non-military scholarship or grant
- Complete a four-year degree and apply to OCS
- Go to college, get a job, and don't join the military at all

While it's important to consider as wide a range of issues and options as possible, it's difficult and sometimes confusing to sort through all the data to arrive at a meaningful conclusion that works for you. One good technique is a Force Field Analysis.[1]

Force Field Analysis builds on the classic "pro and con" list. On the left are "Positive Forces," ones that argue for the proposed decision; on the right are "Negative Forces," ones that argue against it. For each item you put in one column or another, add a weighting factor (1=little importance; 5=critical factor) that describes how important it is to you.

You should do two force field studies: one of the choice to go to an academy, and a second one about any alternate choice you're considering. It's often the case that both options have strengths and weaknesses, so be sure you're as thorough in analyzing whether you should try to go to an academy as whether you should do something else.

Table 2-2 shows a sample force field analysis.

Table 2-2. Force Field Analysis

Positive Forces ⇒	⇐ Negative Forces
Go to a Service Academy	
Serve my country (4)	Plebe-year harassment (2)
Free/low-cost education (3)	Regimentation (2)
Desire to be an officer (3)	Fear of failure (4)
Employment after graduation (3)	Workload/demands (3)
TOTAL = 13	**TOTAL = 11**
Go to a Civilian College or University	
Greater freedom (3)	Higher tuition and fees (5)
Lack of service commitment (3)	Lack of structure (2)
Don't have to take STEM courses (2)	No job guarantee (3)
Can join a fraternity/sorority (1)	Greater temptations (4)
TOTAL = 9	**TOTAL = 14**

The value of exercises like these doesn't come from the numbers you produce, but from the thinking that you put in. Don't automatically conclude that the number you get is a definitive answer. Numbers aren't decisions—they're decision inputs.

Take a close look at every aspect of your analysis. For positive factors, are there ways to make them even more positive? Are there negative aspects of a generally positive factor that you should consider? For negative factors, are there ways to weaken them, either to make them less negative or less important? Are there positive elements of a generally negative factor you should consider? Have you thought of everything? Are there additional factors, either positive or negative, that you should consider? Don't forget that feelings change over time; your answer today may not be the same as your answer three months from now.

Take your decision seriously. It's worth the time and effort to get it right.

3

Getting Ready to Apply

The earliest you can officially start your application process to get into a service academy varies by academy but is no earlier than the beginning of the second semester of your junior year in high school. The specific date for each year is listed on each academy's website as well as in this book's free PDF update (www.militaryacademy.info). Preparation for going to an academy, however, needs to start long before you open your application file.

In this chapter, we'll discuss various ways you can build your file to demonstrate that you have what it takes to be a successful cadet or midshipman. Although we're focusing exclusively on service academies in this book, the things you do to make yourself an outstanding candidate for a service academy will generally also keep you in good standing for the civilian colleges and universities you may also be considering.

START EARLY

In the spring of my son's junior year, he received an email from West Point laying out the steps he needed to take to get his application file squared away and encouraging him to get it done as early as possible. As you'll see later on, there are some significant advantages to having everything done ahead of the pack.

Of course, everything that goes on your college application (service academy or otherwise) is history—what you have done rather than what you're going to do. The bulk of that history has to have been earned before you can get very far in your application process. My son effectively began his quest before he got into high school, years before he was allowed to open up his application file. He managed his high school career, both in and out of school itself, with his goal in mind. He had his fair share of distractions and occasional bouts of procrastination just like any other teenager, of course. Still, he worked harder than he might have worked if he hadn't had the goal. The grades he needed to make to keep his parents off his back were definitely lower than the grades he needed to make to impress West Point. In other words, goals are powerful things. People who know what they want have a real advantage over people who don't.

In this chapter, we'll describe all the ways you can build your credentials so that by the time you start your application, you're most of the way there already.

ADVICE FOR LATE STARTERS

Yes, there's a real advantage to starting early, but what if you don't decide that's what you want to do until later in your high school career—or even after you've graduated from high school? Do you have a chance?

Yes, you do. One person we know didn't decide he wanted to go to an academy until he had already finished two years of college! He made it, graduated, served his military obligation, and today is the US president for a large international corporation.

While the advantage of starting early is real, it's not insurmountable.

There are two situations that may apply to late starters. Let's say your high school record was already exemplary, even though you weren't aiming at an academy at the time. You went to a civilian college and then decided you wanted to go to an academy. If you've got the grades, the sports, and the extracurriculars, you're fine. Just make sure you meet the application deadlines, especially for the Congressional nomination process.

What if your grades were never that great and your athletic and service résumé is spotty? It's not too late to change things. You may need to delay your plans by a year or two so you can get your game up. You might go to another school, take ROTC, and apply a year or two later. (The catch is that you always start at an academy as a plebe, no matter how much prior education you may have.) You could enlist in the military and apply for the competitive exam to go to an academy. You can even get to an academy via the National Guard. Don't forget the prep schools, if you've generally got what it takes but need more academic preparation.

When you get interviewed, expect them to ask about anything unusual in your background and be prepared with your answer. Being asked a hard question isn't a penalty, it's an opportunity to help the academy or the Congressional nominating committee learn who you are.

Always remember that determination counts. When it's clear you really want to go to an academy, people notice.

SPECIAL SITUATIONS

There are various reasons why you may have difficulties in acquiring the academic, athletic, and extracurricular leadership experience you need to be competitive for an academy appointment. People who have experienced economic deprivation or overcome hardship, people who have had nontraditional education (homeschooling, etc.), and people who have been in certain kinds of trouble may feel that they're out of the running because their lives don't fit the typical pattern.

None of these factors will necessarily keep you from winning an academy appointment. Chapter 6 covers a variety of special situations and circumstances, and shows you how to address each one.

THE "WHOLE PERSON" EVALUATION PROCESS

Regular colleges and universities exist to develop students for a variety of occupations and lifestyles. Service academies have a narrower mission: to create leaders for their respective services. When they decide whom to admit or reject, they take into account the needs of the service. If you need glasses, West Point will accommodate you as long as your corrected vision is within limits. The Naval Academy, however, needs to provide a certain number of pilot candidates, so they limit the number of glasses-wearing midshipmen they admit each year. (We'll discuss physical requirements and potential disqualification factors in chapter 7.)

Those factors aside, the academies look for people who are well rounded. You don't have to be equally great at everything, but you've got to meet at least the minimum standards across the board. Excellence in one area won't excuse too great a deficiency in another. That's why service academies use a "whole person" evaluation approach.

Certainly, great grades and SAT/ACT scores matter a lot, but so does athletics. A varsity letter isn't officially mandatory—but over 90 percent of the incoming class has one. Leadership experience and community service matter. It's often hard for high school students to find opportunities to lead, so it's important to be creative. There are leadership roles in student government, sports (team captain is good), student groups (yearbook, newspaper, club president), church groups, and Scouting. If you're an Eagle Scout or Gold Award Scout, that earns points as well.

Measurement

The academy admissions process favors things that can be *counted* or *measured*. Grade point average (GPA), class rank, and standardized test scores are all measurements. You can count such things as varsity letters, honor societies, awards, and offices held. Make sure everything is listed in your academy application.

If there's measurement, there are usually standards or norms. In the case of the academies, they all publish class profiles each year that contain such information as average GPA, test scores, and other information. Use those profiles (see appendix II as well as the PDF update) to benchmark yourself. If you've got some scores below average, you may want to work harder on those areas, but don't despair. "Average" means a lot of people get admitted with numbers lower than the mean.

Point System

With all the emphasis on measurement, it won't surprise you that the academies use a point system to rank the candidates. Of course, the exact list of categories and the points available for each is secret, but you can still get a general idea how it works.

Your "whole person" score is based 60 percent on your academic achievement, 30 percent on your leadership potential, and 10 percent on your physical aptitude. (Chapter 7 covers the physical part.) The academic and leadership categories, in particular, get broken into lots of subcategories. Fortunately, we don't really need to know exactly what they are or how many points are associated with them as long as we can get a general sense of how it works.

On our family's first visit to West Point, we attended a briefing by the admissions department, got a tour, and at the end had the opportunity to sit down with an admissions officer to go over the candidate file. The issue of points came up three times: First, the weighted GPA was added. "Well, *that* gave you a few points," he said. When the subject of volunteer and community service came up, he said, "You're maxed out in that category. If you could become a team captain for some sport, that would help more."

He also looked at my son's SAT scores, did a quick calculation on a piece of scratch paper, and said, "If you could get those scores up about 20 points, that would help as well." After I got home, I looked up the SAT score ranges. An additional 20 points would move my son up exactly 1 percent in the national rankings.

SPECIAL NOTE! There is a maximum point score available for each subcategory. If you've achieved a lot in a single area, it may be smarter to work on other areas instead.

SHOULDERING A HEAVY LOAD

Is it challenging to juggle sports, leadership, academics, and everything else that makes you a competitive candidate? Yes—but that's the point. You'll be challenged in the same way (at a more intense level) when you're at an academy. Showing you can handle it in high school helps demonstrate your ability to handle it later in life.

During the briefing session on our first West Point visit, someone asked if it was better for a candidate to take a very challenging class and get a B, or to take an easier class and get an A. The answer? "We'd prefer that you take the challenging class and get an A."

If that feels like a lot of pressure, again, it's meant to be. You'll have to work hard and work under pressure at an academy, and it's never too early to start practicing. You don't have to be a straight-A student to get into an academy (my son wasn't), but the academies would like to see that you've not only taken on hard challenges, but have done well with them.

Time Management and Study Habits

In today's busy world, time management is essential. If you're trying to get into an academy, it's even more essential. Getting great grades isn't enough; you have to get them efficiently. Learn how to organize, how to schedule, and how to study. If this is a challenge area for you, your high school may have resources to help. You can also find any number of tutors or coaches that help students develop good study and time-management skills. There are books that teach these skills as well. Appendix III contains a list.

My high school offered a class in speed reading. Both my brother and I thought it was one of the most valuable classes we ever took.

Balance

Does this mean you need to abandon your social life, give up any hope of dating, and never do anything fun? Of course not. A healthy life needs friendship, fun, and the occasional video game. The key, both as a candidate and as a cadet or midshipman, is balance. That's another reason time management and study habits are so crucial.

ACADEMICS

As we've noted, 60 percent of your score is based on your academic record. That includes your grades and GPA (don't forget to note whether your GPA is weighted or unweighted), your high school class rank, academic honors or awards, and standardized test scores.

Grades and Class Rank

What kind of grades do you need to get into a service academy? While higher is definitely better, you can get a sense of where you stand by taking a look at the published information of the makeup of each incoming academy class. We've collected a set of them in appendix II. You'll notice that each academy chooses to report different information in different formats, so pay attention to all the class profiles, not merely those of the academies you want to go to. Numbers are reasonably similar from academy to academy, so if your academy hasn't revealed a specific piece of information, you may be able to estimate it from data supplied by another academy.

Only the US Coast Guard Academy reports GPA information, and in their class make up, 95 percent of admitted students have at least a 3.0, and 30 percent have a weighted GPA that exceeds 4.0. The problem with GPA is that high schools vary greatly in their resources and in the demographics of their surrounding communities. A letter grade of B at a top-rated, academically challenging high school can mean more than an A someplace else. Recognizing this, the Air Force Academy website states that adjustments will be made to your academic standing if you attend an unusually competitive school or one in which honors and Advanced Placement (AP) classes don't receive additional weight in calculation of class rank or GPA.

All the academies make this kind of adjustment, so no matter which academy you're targeting, ask your high school guidance counselor to include a profile of the previous year's high school graduating class along with your transcript if your high school falls into one of those categories.

In general, the academies focus more on class rank than overall GPA. It balances out some of the differences among high schools and measures something else that's very important: how well do you stack up against your peer group? At West Point, about 70 percent of admitted students are in the top 20 percent of their high school classes. The Coast Guard reports that 50 percent of their students are in the top 10 percent of their high school classes, and 85 percent in the top 25 percent.

This implies that if you're in the top 20 to 25 percent of your high school class, you're academically acceptable, depending on your other qualifications. On a practical level, you should target being in the top 10 percent to be competitive. The Air Force Academy mentions that while you're required to rank in the top 40 percent of your class, the average of recent entering classes is top 3 percent.

You will be asked for class rank information as part of your academy application. Don't know what your class rank is? Ask your guidance counselor as soon as possible. You may find out that your high school doesn't provide class rank information at all. If so, see the Special Note below.

SPECIAL NOTE! Not all high schools provide class rank. The academies know this and have a process for handling it. It will not adversely affect your prospects for admission. If your school doesn't class rank, be sure to tell your guidance counselor that you are applying to an academy so he or she will be prepared when an inquiry arrives. Tell your academy liaison officer as well. Check the detailed instructions when you are completing the actual application for what to do if your school does not provide class ranking.

Academic Honors

About 10 percent of admitted students to the academies are either valedictorians or salutatorians of their high school classes. Around 60 percent are members of a national honor society. (Again, these numbers are extrapolated from the published class profiles where not all academies report in the same way.) These kinds of honors accompany an outstanding GPA, so you normally don't have to do separate work to qualify.

What Courses Should You Take?

The academies list the specific minimum courses they'd like to see on your high school transcript, summarized in table 3-1. If offered by your school, take honors, Advanced Placement (AP), or International Baccalaureate (IB) level courses, or at a minimum the most rigorous and advanced classes available to you. You may also take courses at local community colleges while in high school to make up for any academic shortcomings in your basic education. (If you are home-schooled, see chapter 6.)

Table 3-1. What Courses You Should Take in High School

Subject	Requirements
English	4 years, emphasis on composition, grammar, literature, and speech. If your school offers a college preparatory class in writing, take it (USAFA).
Mathematics	4 years, including algebra, geometry, intermediate algebra, and trigonometry. If your school offers them, take precalculus and calculus. (USAFA says, "A solid foundation in algebra is more valuable than exposure to calculus," but both is better.) USMMA only requires 3 years of mathematics.
Foreign Language	2 years. USAFA specifies "modern" foreign language. USMMA does not list a foreign language requirement.
Laboratory Science	USMA and USNA: 2 years (the Naval Academy specifies chemistry and physics). USAFA: 4 years, including chemistry, physics, and biology.
History/ Social Studies	1 year of US history, including courses in geography, government, and economics (USMA), plus 1 year of world or European history (USNA). USAFA requires 3 years of history or social studies, including 1 year of US history. USCGA and USMMA do not list a specific history requirement.
Other topics	If your school offers a class in basic computing, take it. USMMA also values courses in mechanical drawing and machine shop, and mentions business courses (economics and statistics), engineering-based courses, and other technical subjects as highly desirable.

Test Scores

As with many colleges and universities, standardized test scores play a large role in whether you get it. If you have an opportunity to take a test prep class, do so. If not, look for online and book resources to help you practice.

You may take either the SAT or ACT examination (for the ACT, you must take the writing portion), and you may take them as many times as you like. The tests have some differences, and some students do much better on one than the other.[1]

> **SPECIAL NOTE!** Nonstandard or special accommodation tests, including untimed or extended time tests, won't be considered.

The academies *superscore* your SAT and ACT results, meaning they take the best score from each category from all the times you took the test. Table 3-2 is an illustration of superscoring. Here, the candidate took the SAT three different times, and earned the scores shown. Of the three reading scores, Test B was highest, so that's the one that counts. For math, Test B was highest, and for writing, Test C won.

Table 3-2. Superscoring

Test Session	SAT Reading	SAT Math	SAT Writing	Superscore Result
Test Session A	627	**655**	608	655
Test Session B	**650**	630	615	650
Test Session C	575	640	**635**	635
Combined SAT Score	1852	1925	1858	**1940**

Table 3-3 lists the codes for submitting test scores to the academies. Your member of Congress and senators also have reporting codes for SAT and ACT scores, which you'll need as part of the nomination process. Those codes will be available in the Congressional nomination application packet.

Table 3-3.   Codes for Submitting Test Scores

Academy	SAT Code	ACT Code
West Point	2934	2976
Naval Academy	5809	1742
Coast Guard Academy	5807	0600
Merchant Marine Academy	Submitted by your high school	
Air Force Academy	4830	0530

Other Tests

The academies don't require any other standardized tests. If you're taking subject matter SAT tests or other special exams as part of applying to other colleges, there's nothing wrong with having copies of the scores sent to your academy, but in most cases they won't carry a lot of weight.

PSAT/NMSQT. Because you can start your candidate file as early as January of your junior year in high school, you might not have taken the SAT or ACT yet. In that case, you can use your score on the Preliminary Scholastic Aptitude Test/National Merit Scholarship Qualifying Test (PSAT/NMSQT) to prequalify as a candidate (see chapter 4) or to apply to the academy summer program, discussed later in this chapter. These test scores will not count in your overall candidate evaluation.

Advanced Placement Examinations. If you take Advanced Placement (AP) classes in high school, you can take the corresponding AP exam and potentially exempt yourself from some entry-level college classes. Do submit any AP scores, especially scores of 4 or 5. The academies normally test new cadets and midshipmen during Cadet Basic Training to determine whether you place out of any first-year classes, but consider high AP scores in making their decision.

ATHLETICS

Athletics can give you points both in the physical portion of your "whole person" evaluation and also in the leadership category. A varsity letter, for example, doesn't merely mean that you have the minimum necessary ability to play a varsity level sport, but also recognizes leadership, discipline, hard work, and character.

Varsity Letter

The vast majority of cadets and midshipmen have a varsity letter in some high school sport, ranging from 79 percent at the Air Force Academy to 94 percent at West Point. Unless you're playing a non–high school sport at a competitive level, you should plan to earn a varsity letter. It's easier to get varsity letters at some high schools than others, and it's easier in some sports than others. Talk to your head coach about your ambitions and ask what you need to do to earn that letter.

Which Sports?

West Point, the Naval Academy, and the Air Force Academy are NCAA Division I schools, and the Coast Guard Academy and the Merchant Marine Academy are in Division III. Like most colleges and universities, the service academies actively recruit student athletes. Unlike most colleges and universities, there isn't a lot of extra financial benefit, because everyone gets a full scholarship. For more on recruited athletes, see chapter 6.

If you don't think you're going to stand out as top material for one of the academy teams, then play the sport or sports you like, as long as they're at the varsity level.

Some people may play competitive varsity level sports that aren't affiliated with a school. If you're in a travel soccer league, compete in martial arts tournaments, or run marathons, those count too, even if they can't give you a varsity letter. Be prepared to provide information about the sport, and in particular list any honors, trophies, or other recognition that makes you stand apart.

Team Captain

Over 60 percent of cadets and midshipmen were captains or co-captains of their team, and that's worth specific points on your evaluation. Let your coaches and teammates know about your ambitions, and make sure you earn the role.

Awards and Honors

Awards, honors, trophies, and other recognition testify to your skill, leadership, and character. Remember, though, that not all trophies are created equal, and burying your application in every minor trophy you ever got isn't necessarily to your advantage. Pick the best and the most prestigious, and look for opportunities to earn more recognition.

EXTRACURRICULAR ACTIVITIES

In addition to great grades and athletic achievement, a well-rounded candidate participates in other activities as well. That doesn't mean join everything you can; a list of twenty school clubs with no leadership roles is worth a lot less than one or two activities or clubs in which you do particularly well.

The class profiles for the various academies break out the number of successful candidates who participated in specific types of high

SPECIAL NOTE! Focus your attention on just a few areas; don't try to be everything. Being a mover and a shaker in a single activity means a lot more than being a participant in twenty.

Table 3-4. High School Activities in Academy Class Profiles

Activity	USMA	USNA	USCGA	USMMA	USAFA
Student Body Leadership	18% (class/ student body president)	69% (student body leader)	49% (student council or club officer)	Not reported	18% (class president/VP)
Dramatics, Public Speaking, or Debating	13% debate, 10% drama	67%	Not reported	Not reported	Not reported
Student Publications	18% (newspaper editor/staff), 8% yearbook editor/co-editor)	11%	Not reported	Not reported	Not reported
Music (Band/ Chorus Member)	Not reported	30%	30%	Not reported	Not reported
Tutoring	Not reported	46%	Not reported	Not reported	Not reported

school activities, and it's worth reviewing what academies single out. Table 3-4 summarizes that data; the full tables are located in appendix II. Note that the academies break out categories with a lot of students in them; don't be concerned if your leadership strengths lie elsewhere.

Student Government

One concept you'll hear during the applications process is "peer leadership," the idea that you have been chosen by your fellow students, club members, or team members to be a leader. Student government is a great place to demonstrate that your fellow students consider you a leader, and the skills of running a successful political campaign, even at a high school level, are valuable.

Dramatics, Public Speaking, or Debating

While the relationship of public speaking and debating to the skills of being a great officer are fairly clear, you might wonder how dramatics figures into the process.

There was a famous military rivalry between General Dwight Eisenhower and General Douglas MacArthur. As a colonel, Eisenhower had served as MacArthur's chief of staff, and the two had a very serious falling out. From that time on, MacArthur normally described Eisenhower as "the best company clerk I ever had."

Eisenhower got his revenge. When some years later, a reporter asked if he knew Douglas MacArthur, Ike replied, "I studied dramatics under him for seven years!"[2]

Eisenhower wasn't the first person to point out MacArthur's dramatic ability, and for all their rivalry, it was in some ways a compliment. Even a brief look at military history will show that generals (and admirals) can be very colorful characters, and sometimes that's part of their success.

You should know how to craft a clear, well-researched argument. You should be able to stand up in front of a large group of people, command their attention, and deliver your message. And just a touch of showmanship at the right moment can make it all come together.

Publications

Because communication is such a key part of leadership, experience working on student publications helps demonstrate your ability to research, write, edit, and display information. Officers write reports, conduct briefings, and prepare presentations. In addition to showing communications skills, reporting can often show investigatory or analytical skills, and an editorial role counts toward leadership. Awards for reporting, writing, investigating, and design should also be mentioned, even if they are awarded to the entire publication rather than to you as an individual.

Science, Technology, Engineering, Math (STEM)

Interestingly, the class profile breakdowns don't show involvement in science, technology, engineering, or mathematics (STEM) activities, but all the academies have a strong STEM orientation. No matter what major you select, you'll end up with at least an engineering minor, which is why every academy graduate receives a bachelor of science (BS) degree.

Under "What Courses Should You Take" above, we listed the specific science requirements for academies, but you should think of those as minimums. Unfortunately, not all high schools offer the same range of opportunities to students, but if your high school offers engineering or other technical courses, they will help.

Does your school have a computer club? A robotics club? Science fair? Even if your military or career ambitions don't primarily lie in the STEM field, they are such a strong part of the core curriculum and are so fundamental to your success in the field that you should try to demonstrate your aptitude and interest in these areas both academically and on an extracurricular basis.

Tutoring

Only the Naval Academy breaks out tutoring as a specific category, but they show that 46 percent of the incoming class had done at least some tutoring. As always, it's reasonable to assume the numbers for other academies are similar. Tutoring shows leadership, communications ability, and community service, and need not take that many hours of your time.

Club Leadership

In addition to leadership roles for the student body or your class as a whole, there are also numerous leadership opportunities available in various school clubs. It's better to be a leader in one club than a member of eight, so focus your interests where you can achieve the best results. It's not necessary that the clubs you choose have a direct military application. The academies themselves have a wide range of clubs and activities for cadets and midshipmen, not all of which are oriented toward military skills.

Start Your Own Club

If you don't find a club that matches your interests and aptitudes, you can consider starting one. Being the founder of a club gives you points in addition to any leadership role. My son started a club in his high school for students considering military service, and invited various recruiters to speak to interested students after school. There are normally procedures you need to follow to create a club and have it recognized by your school, including finding a faculty sponsor. Check with the principal's office or the guidance office for details.

OPPORTUNITIES OUTSIDE SCHOOL

You don't have to limit yourself to official in-school activities; many wonderful opportunities are available elsewhere.

Academy Summer Programs

All of the academies except for Merchant Marine offer a week-long summer program for interested high school juniors. These programs offer a great opportunity for candidates to get a first-hand taste of academy life. Naturally, they're very competitive, so apply early. These programs carry a cost, tuition plus travel plus incidental expenses. There may be financial aid available in some hardship cases; check with the respective academy. (The Naval Academy offers a Summer STEM Program for rising ninth, tenth, and eleventh graders as well, but this is not a simulation of academy life.)

Table 3-5 summarizes information on the academy summer programs.

Table 3-5. Academy Summer Programs

USMA Summer Leader Experience (SLE). Cost: $400. Must be a high school junior (current year), be a US citizen, reach the age of seventeen before the year in which you would become a USMA freshman, and have a valid PSAT, PLAN, SAT, or ACT test score. The first part of the SLE application is the same as Part I of the USMA applications process, which opens your candidate file. You must then apply specifically for SLE. For information: www.usma.edu/admissions/sitepages/summer.aspx.

USNA Summer Seminar. Cost: $450. Must be unmarried, not pregnant, and without legal obligation to support a child. Superior high school performance (GPA and test scores), athletic and extracurricular activities, physically fit, vision 20/40 or correctable to 20/20. US citizenship is not a requirement for summer seminar, but it is a requirement for admission to the academy. Applying to Summer Seminar also functions as the preliminary USNA application; don't submit both. For information: www.usna.edu/Admissions/Programs/NASS/index.php.

USNA Summer STEM Program. Cost: $425. The Summer STEM Program at the Naval Academy is designed to encourage students to pursue STEM education through high school and college, and is open to students entering ninth through eleventh grade. Unlike the other programs mentioned here, it is not designed to introduce candidates to academy life. For information: www.usna.edu/Admissions/Programs/STEM/index.php.

USCGA Academy Introduction Mission (AIM) Summer Program. Cost: $400. Must be a US citizen, high school junior, sixteen–eighteen years old, good health and physical condition, meet medical requirements. Evaluated by personal statements, high school transcripts, and recommendations. Approximately one-third of recent incoming classes attended AIM. For information: www.cga.edu/admissions2.aspx?id=88.

USAFA Summer Seminar. Cost: $300. Requirements: GPA 2.5 or above, test scores (optional), personal profile. If you have test scores, you can have your summer seminar application also serve as your preliminary Air Force Academy application. For information: www.academyadmissions.com/admissions/outreach-programs/summer-seminar/.

> **SPECIAL NOTE!** While going to an academy summer program can be helpful, it's far from mandatory. There are a lot fewer summer program slots than there are places in the incoming class. Getting into a summer program doesn't mean you'll be accepted by the academy, and not getting in doesn't mean you won't. My son didn't get into the West Point summer program, but clearly that didn't keep him from being appointed.

Boys/Girls State

In reviewing the West Point application timeline calendar for our son's year (see table P-1), we were surprised to find a recommendation that candidates attend Boys or Girls State during the summer following their junior year in high school. This "recommendation" turned out to be a lot more important than we thought. About 18 percent of West Point and about 17 percent of Air Force Academy incoming freshmen were graduates of Boys or Girls State. (The others didn't report a figure.)

> **SPECIAL NOTE!** In general, if you see the words "recommended," "strongly recommended," "strongly encourage," "preferred," or anything similar, you should treat it as if it's just short of mandatory. Unless there is an active reason you cannot, do it.

Although I was vaguely aware that Boys/Girls State existed, I knew very little about it. My son's school guidance office didn't know anything either, so our next stop was the Internet. There's a good Wikipedia article on the program and its history (http://en.wikipedia.org/wiki/Boys/Girls_State), and the main website for the program can be found at www.boysandgirlsstate.org.

Boys State and Girls State are summer leadership programs offered in each state for rising high school seniors sponsored by the American Legion, and they're free to attend. Around twenty thousand students a year attend. There's a Boys/Girls Nation as well, but to go to that you have to be selected as a delegate from your state event.

To get in, you need a nomination from a history teacher and a local chapter of the American Legion to sponsor you. If your initial inquiry doesn't get results, keep looking. In our case, our local American Legion chapter never got back to us, so we started with the state office until we found a chapter just a little farther away that was happy to sponsor our son.

The program itself is a mock state legislature, with the attendees serving as legislators and running for elective office. You get automatic points simply for attending, and if you get elected to a high office (governor, lieutenant governor, senator), that's even better. You don't need the governorship to get into a service academy, but you do need to demonstrate "peer leadership," and getting your fellow attendees to elect you to office is practical evidence that you have the quality they're looking for.

We learned later that Boys/Girls State is so important that if you're faced with a date conflict and you can either attend an academy summer session or Boys/Girls State that you should go with the latter.

On top of that, it's a lot of fun. Of all the summer activities our son participated in, Boys State was his favorite. He got elected governor, which we think was a significant boost to his admission chances, but lots of people get in without that. Remember, there are many different ways to demonstrate that you're the person they want.

Scouting/Sea Cadets/Civil Air Patrol

There's probably a Boy Scout and a Girl Scout troop close to you, and Scouting is a traditional activity for potential cadets and midshipmen. At West Point, about 40 percent of the class have been active in Scouting, with about 13 percent holding the rank of Eagle Scout or Gold Award Scout. If you're in Scouting, it's very much worth your while to pursue your Eagle or Gold Award.

While all the academies recognize the leadership and community service value that comes from Scouting, don't limit your horizons to just the Boy Scouts or Girl Scouts. If you are interested in the Navy, Coast Guard, or Merchant Marine, check out the US Naval Sea Cadet Corps (www.seacadets.org). If flying is your passion, consider the Civil Air Patrol, a US Air Force auxiliary with both adult and teen programs (www.gocivilairpatrol.com/cap_home/teens/).

JROTC

The Junior Reserve Officers' Training Corps (JROTC) is a Federal program for secondary school students. Unlike its senior partner, ROTC, it isn't designed to build military officers directly, but rather to instill in high school students the value of citizenship, service, and personal responsibility. While it's not designed primarily as a recruiting tool, somewhere between 30 percent and 50 percent of JROTC cadets go on to serve in some branch of the military.

As with ROTC, each service operates JROTC units: there are Army, Air Force, Navy, Marine Corps, and Coast Guard flavors, although the vast majority are Army.

There are over three thousand JROTC programs at various high schools, both public and private. Each unit has at least one commissioned or warrant officer and at least one retired non-commissioned officer. Depending on the program, JROTC students have the opportunity to receive between one and four years of instruction, with areas of study including military science, military history, and physical fitness. Often, extracurricular activities, ranging from drill and color guard to rocketry, are available to JROTC cadets. Student can earn rank and various awards.

Of particular interest to service academy candidates is the fact that certain JROTC "honor units with distinction" are able to nominate up to three cadets or midshipmen for the service. (See chapter 5.) In addition to academy nominations, JROTC cadets can qualify for advanced rank if they enlist in the military, although there is no obligation for a JROTC cadet to join the military.

If your school offers JROTC, even if it's not the branch of service you want, it's a good idea to join. In addition to the potential nomination opportunity, it's a good way to get a taste of military service and cadet life.

The problem, of course, is that there are more than twenty-four thousand secondary schools in the United States, so it's quite likely that your school doesn't offer JROTC. It's not fair to penalize candidates who don't have the opportunity to take JROTC, so the lack of that experience doesn't count against you.

Military School

My son originally wanted to go to military school because of his ambition to be in the military. However, a number of students are enrolled in military schools not because of their ambition to serve, but rather to deal with a variety of behavioral or academic deficiencies. If you're thinking of military school as a way to help you qualify for an academy, try to find a school where a large proportion of students are there because they want to be.

A number of military boarding schools offer JROTC, but surprisingly, not all. Some religiously-affiliated schools have difficulty combining the secular JROTC program with the overall emphasis of the school, so elect not to offer it.

Earlier, we mentioned JROTC "honor units with distinction," which are able to offer direct academy nominations. Some private military schools fall into this category, so be sure to check if the school you're considering is one of them.

COMMUNITY SERVICE

Community activities give you leadership opportunities, show character, and demonstrate your interest in service. That's why it's an important part of demonstrating that you are a well-rounded and suitable candidate for admission to an academy. You can do community service through your school (many schools require some community service as part of requirements for graduation), through local government agencies, through churches and other religious groups, through a variety of private organizations, or you can even create your own service opportunity.

Schools

Not only are a certain number of community service hours necessary for graduation from high school in some states, but schools also perform community service work directly, through school clubs, and by providing a clearinghouse of opportunities for students. Start with your guidance office to see what's available.

Government

Government at local, state, and federal levels use volunteers to supplement paid civil servants in delivering certain community services. Police departments sometimes sponsor basketball teams for at-risk youth; local governments may operate facilities for the care of elderly or disabled citizens; hospitals often search out volunteers to provide comfort and support to patients of all ages.

Churches and Religious Groups

Charitable and community service activities are often part of the mission of religious institutions of all faiths and varieties. If you attend a religious institution, consider joining in any youth group activities or charitable work, and seek leadership roles when appropriate. In some cases, you may even have an opportunity to travel internationally to do charitable or community work.

Charity Work

While religious institutions operate any number of charitable programs, there are also charities not directly affiliated with a religious body, and they can usually use motivated, hardworking volunteers.

Environment and Social Services

Perhaps your interests are environmental in nature. Cleaning up parks, mucking out streams, planting trees, and working to preserve nature provide excellent opportunities to demonstrate service, character, and leadership.

Such programs as Habitat for Humanity give you the opportunity to provide meaningful services to people in need and at the same time learn valuable craft skills.

Veterans and Military Support

Many organizations exist to provide services and support to veterans. In addition to volunteering at VA hospitals or being part of a Wounded Warriors project, there are also memorial projects, such as collecting oral histories from veterans of older conflicts, such as World War II.

Volunteer Fire/EMS

I was completely unaware that you can (at least in our area—check the rules where you live) become a volunteer firefighter and Emergency Medical Technician (EMT) at the age of sixteen! Fortunately, my son discovered this, and as soon as he was eligible, applied to become a volunteer at our local fire station. He told me once, "This is as close as I can get to being in the Army without dropping out of high school."

Although the work is unpaid, the demands are very high. James spent the summer following his sophomore year taking the course to get licensed as an EMT, and during the fall semester of his junior year, attended the fire academy one night a week and all day each Saturday to become a certified firefighter.

He fell in love with the work and rode as often as he could (occasionally so much that his parents had to put their foot down and insist he give equal time to schoolwork). When he turned eighteen in the fall of his senior year, he became eligible to be "Charge EMT," in command of the ambulance for his shift.

SPECIAL NOTE! Don't think you have to choose an activity related to the military for maximum credit. The academies care about your leadership and service and don't care particularly where you get it—so choose something you care about. *Passion produces results.* If you choose an activity simply to beef up your résumé, you probably won't give it all you've got. Pick something you care about doing even if you don't think it's directly related to the academy or branch of service you plan to pursue.

Volunteer fire and rescue services can always use highly motivated and hardworking new members. If this is something that interests you, my son and I strongly suggest you check it out.

Create Your Own

When Hurricane Katrina devastated New Orleans, Jackie Kantor, a freshman at Walt Whitman High School in Bethesda, Maryland (the same high school my son attended), and her younger sister Melissa had the idea of giving backpacks filled with useful items to children displaced by Katrina. Armed with a website and some local promotion, they collected and filled over fifty thousand backpacks to be given away, and the story made the national news.[3]

Community service doesn't have to be limited to existing organizations; you can in fact create your own.

LEARNING AND ADVENTURE

Travel

If you've been to twenty-seven countries as a tourist, that's interesting, but it doesn't say very much about who you are as a person. If you've had the opportunity to live and study abroad, if you can claim familiarity with another culture or another language, if you have developed meaningful connections, those things can help you stand out.

Travel can be domestic or international. You can visit big cities, small towns, or remote areas. You can do work, live with people, study, immerse yourself in other cultures, or many other things that do speak to who you are and what you've done.

Outward Bound–type Programs

Of the various programs that offer outdoor experiential learning and adventure opportunities, Outward Bound is the best known, but not the only one. Showing that you can face and overcome physical and environmental challenges is certainly something that academies are likely to find relevant. Depending on the branch of service, you may find programs on the land, at sea, and even in the air—skydiving, for example.

As you know, you'll need to write essays as part of the academy application, in pursuit of your Congressional nomination, and for any other colleges and universities you may be considering. One of the biggest problems young people have in writing these essays is a lack of meaningful life experiences. If you do something challenging, important, or life-changing, one fringe benefit is that you'll have something good to write about.

Summer Programs

Take advantage of your summers to the extent possible. While you certainly need and deserve some downtime, summer vacations are long enough to get your R&R and still have time left over to do something meaningful in support of your academy goal. Your summer efforts can relate to another activity of the sort we've been discussing, or you can use the opportunity to go in a different direction.

College Courses/Continuing Education

If your high school doesn't offer advanced courses such as calculus or computer science, consider taking a class or two at a community college. Sometimes, you can get credit from your high school (and even go to classes during your regular school day).

WORK

You can always get a job and earn some money while doing it. The act of working shows a certain degree of character and self-discipline, even if the job itself isn't particularly impressive. Even if you're just working fast food, you can become a team leader. Leadership is leadership, no matter where you're working.

Of course, if you can get a more impressive position, that's great as well. However, a leadership position at a job with less prestige may be more valuable than a lesser role at a better job. Internships, paid or unpaid, count as well.

If you are working in order to help support your family, see the section in chapter 6 titled "Economically Disadvantaged/Hardship Candidates" and make sure your academy field representative knows your situation. That counts substantially toward the evaluation of your character and leadership ability, as indeed it should.

CHOOSE YOUR OWN ADVENTURE

One of my wife's cousins took a bicycle trip across the United States. In one of my very first post-college jobs, an equally junior colleague of mine got hired because he'd taken a canoe trip down the Rhine River. These adventures didn't relate to the career direction of either person, but that doesn't matter—what the activities said about the person is what mattered, not the activity itself.

You don't have to limit yourself to physical adventure, either. I've known young people who wrote and self-published a book, composed and recorded a CD, created a podcast, and designed a smartphone app. The subject matter isn't nearly as important as the initiative. Think outside the box. You don't have to limit yourself to the official range of organized activities.

4

The Applications Process

The official process of applying to a service academy can begin no earlier than the second half of your junior year in high school. Each academy posts the official dates on its website. The process for all the academies except for Merchant Marine is done online through what is known as your "candidate portal." (The Merchant Marine Academy gives you a choice of applying online or on paper.) You'll become intimately familiar with your portal as you go through the process.

Start by going to the appropriate academy website to begin your journey, using the information in table 4-1. While you can't start applying before the portal opens for your particular class year, it's never too early to visit the site and look around.

Table 4-1. Application Links

Academy	Admissions Portal
West Point	www.usma.edu/admissions/SitePages/Home.aspx
Naval Academy	www.usna.edu/Admissions/
Coast Guard Academy	www.cga.edu/admissions/
Merchant Marine Academy	www.usmma.edu/admissions
Air Force Academy	www.academyadmissions.com

The next sections of this chapter detail the application steps for each academy. Because there's a lot of similarity among the academies, we've covered the first academy in the most detail, and for the other academies we'll focus on the differences. No matter which academy you're pursuing, it's a good idea to be familiar with the entire process.

GENERAL TIPS

You will be amazed at the volume of paperwork generated by your academy application, Congressional (or other) nomination, and medical exam—not to mention all the paperwork that comes after you've been accepted! If you're applying to ROTC and other colleges at the same time, there's even more you need to keep track of.

If you don't have a filing cabinet at home with a spare drawer you can commandeer, buy yourself a file box and plenty of folders. Set up folders for every single part of the process and make sure each document gets into a folder as soon as possible. Don't let the paper pile up; you'll regret it.

Although a lot of the application process will be done online, *print out everything and file it*! If anything gets lost or misplaced, if you don't get in on your first try and need to apply again the following year, or if you're asked questions about anything in your application, you'll want to have everything organized and at your fingertips.

Don't throw the paperwork away even after you get in. Some of it may come back into play when you're eventually applying for graduate school or for any post-military job.

In particular, once you're accepted, you'll have to apply for a security clearance. During your military career, you'll have to renew your clearance from time to time, and may need to get it upgraded from Secret to Top Secret and the various special clearances that can go along with Top Secret. (There's more information about security clearances in chapter 8.) The same form is used for all levels of clearance, and you'll have to update it each time. Having a record of what you submitted earlier will save you tremendous time and headache as you move forward.

Not every applicant is the same, and you may have special issues or considerations that will affect how you go about the applications process. Chapter 6 of this book has information for potential recruited athletes, diversity candidates, homeschooled applicants, and others who may have specific concerns, questions, and issues. If any of these situations apply to you, be sure to read that chapter before beginning your application.

West Point, the Naval Academy, and the Air Force Academy also have free apps available for iPhone and Android. Search the appropriate app store to find them.

The Air Force app will actually allow you to start an application and visit your candidate portal. The Naval Academy will let you find your admissions counselor and see a list of admissions events. Their app has an "Introduce Yourself" button to contact admissions, but at the time of writing, it crashed every time I tried it. It does not allow you to apply or access your portal. The West Point app doesn't have any admissions related functions other than some information sheets and a general checklist.

All these apps will no doubt improve over time, so it's a good idea to get them. While you're visiting your app store, check for other related apps. Cadets and midshipmen are required to know and recite on command such details as upcoming menus and days until graduation. There's an app for that.

SPECIAL NOTE! If you're male and within the age range where you're eligible to apply for an academy, you are still legally required to register for the draft, and you *will* be asked for your Selective Service registration number at some point during the applications process. You can register online at www.sss.gov/regver/wfregistration.aspx.

WEST POINT

The West Point admissions website has a lot of material, and it's a good idea to download and study the information they provide before clicking the link to start your application. There are links to an overall timeline, admissions events in your area, FAQs, and a very useful set of admissions tips. There are special links with information for high school seniors, juniors, middle school students, active and reserve soldiers, international cadets (see chapter 5), diversity outreach, and much more.

Preliminary Application

Applications usually open in January of what will typically be your junior year. To begin your application, click www.usma.edu/admissions/SitePages/Apply.aspx. The first thing you'll see is a window where you can enter your name, social security number, date of birth, and high school graduation year. The site checks that you meet the necessary age requirements and whether you already have an open file.

The next window is your preliminary application. In addition to basic information such as name and address, they'll want your class rank (if your school doesn't provide class ranks, follow the instructions), any test scores, athletic and non-athletic activities, whether you have served in the military, a few health questions, and informa-

tion on other colleges or ROTC scholarships for which you're applying. You'll also have a chance to apply to West Point's Summer Leadership Experience (SLE) program if you're a high school junior.

Once you submit your preliminary application, you'll get an email
with a West Point ID number and a temporary password. Use that information to log on to the candidate portal at https://candidate.usma.
edu/. You'll be asked to create a new password, and you're in.

Your initial status will read "Initial Evaluation Pending." The
West Point Admissions team will review the information you provide
to determine whether you are a competitive candidate for admission.
If West Point decides you aren't a competitive candidate, you're finished for this year, but you can reapply next year.

Initial evaluations for next year's class can't begin until the admissions team finishes with this year's class. Except for determining
whether you will be selected to attend SLE, the admissions team may
not look at your application until late June or July.

> **SPECIAL NOTE!** You can update your preliminary application with new information,
> such as additional test scores and other activities, up until the admissions team makes
> their initial evaluation. It's very much to your advantage to give the admissions team
> every possible reason to see you as a viable candidate.

Summer Leadership Experience

If you are selected to attend SLE, you'll be notified by email and
through the portal. Check the portal regularly, as emails have been
known to get lost. If you are selected for SLE, there will be a package
of information and forms for you to download.

Regional Commanders and Liaison Officers

Before we get to the details of the candidate portal, there are some very
important people you need to know as you go through the applications
process. These include the Regional Commander, the State Coordinator, and the Liaison Officer for your Congressional district.

For admissions purposes, the country is divided into five regions,
with a Regional Commander in charge of all candidates that come
from those regions. Regional Commanders are located at West Point.
They will evaluate and rank candidates from each region, decide on
medical waivers (see chapter 7), and generally oversee the process.
You can find the name and contact information for your Regional

Commander on the West Point website. Once you have access to your candidate portal, the information will be accessible there as well.

Each Congressional district has a Liaison Officer, also known as a Field Force Representative, and there is a State Coordinator for each state. State Coordinators and Liaison Officers are either active duty or reserve officers who volunteer their time to provide support to candidates from their areas. Most, but not all, are West Point graduates themselves. They participate in various recruiting activities, work with candidates in their areas, and conduct the formal West Point interview as part of your admissions process.

Field Force Representatives can be of tremendous help in the process, and it's a good idea to make contact early. Send an email to your liaison officer to introduce yourself, and use the liaison officer as support through the admissions process. If you have issues that your liaison officer can't (or won't) help you with, you can also contact your State Coordinator or your Regional Commander. You'll find that people in the admissions chain of command are quite responsive and willing to help. Before you ask a question, check the website or other information to see if you can find the answer on your own. If your issue isn't covered, or if the information is unclear or doesn't quite describe your situation, don't hesitate to get in touch.

Your Field Force Representative will often visit you to have a preliminary discussion about the academy and then again to conduct your formal admissions interview when you reach that point in the process.

SPECIAL NOTE! Everybody has a Liaison Officer/Field Force Representative, a State Coordinator, and a Regional Commander to call on. There are also Diversity Outreach Officers (chapter 6) for each region, as well as officers for reserve candidates, active military candidates, National Guard candidates, and recruited athletes, all within the West Point admission office. If you fall into any of these categories, check the West Point website to find out who your particular contacts are, and contact them with any issues or special concerns that you can't resolve on your own by checking the website.

Candidate Portal

You'll be notified by email once the initial evaluation is finished, and if you're considered competitive, you'll then be able to log on to the Candidate Portal to continue the process. If you have persistent problems logging on, send an email to your Regional Commander.

Your candidate portal will now list everything that needs to be done. Each item will be marked with a status icon, and your job is to turn all the red icons into green ones. Some icons turn green auto-

> **SPECIAL NOTE!** Check your candidate portal often, especially as you get further along in the process. Even though some items (such as references) need to be completed by other people, you are ultimately responsible for following up and making sure everything happens. Until all the status icons turn green, the academy can't offer you admission.

matically when particular bits of information (such as test scores) get into the system, but most require some action on your part.

Once your candidate portal opens up, be sure to download the various PDFs provided. You'll find a list of regional contacts, an instruction booklet, and height and weight standards. To the right, you'll see a list of all the information that needs to be in your "Candidate Kit."

You'll provide some of the information in your kit personally. Other information will be sent in by various people, ranging from test companies to references to the person who administers your Candidate Fitness Assessment (chapter 7).

Rather than send in hard copy, you'll generally scan and upload documents to the system. They won't always appear on your portal immediately. The instructions tell you to allow up to three weeks. If the documents don't appear, first make sure that they were properly sent (and if not, resend them), and if they were properly sent, send a brief email to your Regional Commander. Attach a copy of the missing document.

Candidate Kit Contents

Candidate Personal Data Record. This is basic information, such as name, address, date of birth, height, weight, gender, and so on.

Official ACT or SAT Scores. These are sent in by the testing company, using the school's ID number. See "Test Scores" in chapter 3 for school codes and information on superscoring. Remember, you can (and should) take the tests multiple times; see also the discussion of ACT versus SAT. While you'll be asked for your PSAT on the preliminary application (many juniors won't yet have taken the SAT or ACT yet), that's for SLE consideration and initial assessment. PSAT scores don't count toward the final decision.

High School Transcripts. Because most applicants won't have finished high school, you'll normally submit a six-semester transcript initially, and submit the seventh- and eighth-semester transcripts as they become available. These need to be official transcripts sent by your school. Your final transcript won't be sent in until after the deci-

SPECIAL NOTE! Be sure to specify whether your GPA is weighted or unweighted.

sion is made, so those final grades don't count quite as much. However, if your grades take a nosedive, the academy may withdraw its offer. (A couple of Cs wouldn't be a problem; but a D or F could be fatal.)

Candidate Activities Record. You'll fill in your contact information and then get access to the entire form. You may need to update this as your high school career continues.

Candidate Statements. Just like normal schools, the academies do want essays. The topics in my son's year were "Why I want to attend West Point" and "My commitment to diversity." There's a discussion on essays in chapter 5, "Getting a Nomination."

SPECIAL NOTE! Take your required essays seriously, but don't go nuts. Remember that admissions teams will read thousands of these statements each year, and they won't be going over them line by line. Substance counts more than style. Examples mean more than generalities. Be brief, clear, and to the point. Typos and grammatical errors have a way of jumping out, so make sure what you submit is free of errors.

Candidate Fitness Assessment. The CFA is discussed in detail in chapter 7. For the candidate portal, you will first find someone willing and qualified to administer the test and enter his or her contact information. That person will then receive an email with detailed instructions and a link to a webpage to upload your scores.

Supplemental Information Sheet. The Supplemental Information Sheet is primarily intended for applicants who have graduated high school and attended a year or more of college. If so, you'll use this space to add any additional athletic participation and extracurricular activities.

Employer's Evaluation of Candidate. If you have work experience, you'll need to arrange for your manager or supervisor to complete an evaluation form, which you can download from the portal.

SPECIAL NOTE! Although the Supplemental Information Sheet is aimed at post–high school applicants, it's not limited to that purpose. If there's anything important that you want the admissions team to consider that doesn't fit into another part of the applications process, enter it here. If you aren't sure whether the additional information is important, talk it over with your Field Force Representative. If it's a toss-up, add it anyway.

School Official Evaluations. You will need to arrange for three teachers to write evaluations on your behalf. These *must* be from one English teacher, one math teacher, and one physics or chemistry teacher. These are not optional, and you can't substitute teachers of other subjects. It's a good idea to approach teachers early. During senior year, teachers are asked to prepare evaluations and write recommendations for a large number of college-bound students, and there's a limit as to how many they can handle. Get ahead of the crowd and line up your references now. And please be sure to pick teachers who think highly of you!

As with the CFA, you'll enter the teacher contact information and the teacher will get an email with the appropriate forms and links to submit their evaluations.

> **SPECIAL NOTE!** While the English, math, and physics/chemistry evaluations are mandatory, you are permitted to submit additional ones if you want. If you are planning to major in history or international relations, say, a glowing evaluation from a history teacher could be helpful.

Medical. In chapter 7, we'll go through the medical clearance process step by step. As far as your candidate portal is concerned, no exam will be scheduled until you've provided most of the application information and West Point has decided you're a competitive candidate. As soon as that happens (the earlier, the better), you'll be given instructions on scheduling your exam through the candidate portal. The portal will also record current status of your exam process. The examining agency, known as DoDMERB (Department of Defense Medical Evaluation Review Board) has its own candidate portal, which we will cover later.

Nominations. The next chapter will discuss applying for nominations. Once you obtain a nomination, that information will show up on your portal. If you've been notified by your Congressional representative that you have been nominated, check your portal to be sure the information shows up there, and if not, follow up with the Congressional office (or other nominating source) and your Field Force Representative. You can also send an email (with a copy of any nomination letter or other documentation you've received) to your Regional Commander.

Prep School

The United States Military Academy Preparatory School (USMAPS) is for people who are otherwise well qualified but need additional academic preparation. There is no separate application for the prep school; you're automatically considered if you don't get into the academy itself. If you are offered a USMAPS appointment, you'll attend for one very intensive year. While you aren't guaranteed admission to the academy, if you do well at USMAPS your chances of an appointment are very good.

Prep school appointments at all the academies work the same way.

NAVAL ACADEMY

Begin the process by visiting the Naval Academy Admissions website at www.usna.edu/Admissions/. As with the West Point website, start by familiarizing yourself with the site. In particular, look for any admissions forums or events that will be held in your area; they are a great opportunity to get more information and to meet people who can help you in your quest.

Summer Seminar and Preliminary Application

At the time of writing (March 2015), applications for the Class of 2020 will not open until April 1 of this year. However, you can apply for Summer Semester, the Naval Academy's six-day summer program for high school juniors, beginning in January. Summer Semester at the Naval Academy is the equivalent of West Point's Summer Leadership Experience (SLE). Your Summer Semester application also serves as your Preliminary Application, which gets you into their system early.

If you're selected for Summer Semester, that's a pretty good indication that you are indeed competitive. However, if you aren't selected for Summer Semester, that doesn't mean you *won't* be found competitive. Every year, a number of people who didn't get into the summer program for their academy eventually are offered admission, and some people who did get into the summer program don't make it into the academy.

In addition, the Naval Academy offers the Summer STEM Program for students interested in science, technology, engineering, and mathematics. This program has a separate application, and it *does not* count as your Preliminary Application. There are sessions for rising ninth, tenth, and eleventh graders. The STEM program doesn't simulate academy life, and it's aimed at a wider audience than people who specifically want to attend the Naval Academy.

Find links to both applications at www.usna.edu/Admissions/Programs/index.php.

Blue and Gold Officers and Other Admission Staff

You'll see a link on the Admissions home page labeled "Blue and Gold Officers (BGIS)." These are the equivalent of West Point's Field Force Representatives, liaison officers who handle candidates in each Congressional district. State Coordinators are known as Blue and Gold Officer Area Coordinators; a list of them can be found here: www .usna.edu/Admissions/BGO/. If you're having trouble finding or getting access to your Blue and Gold Officer, send an email to the Area Coordinator for your state.

Blue and Gold Officers and Area Coordinators, like their West Point counterparts, are volunteers. Regional Directors, like West Point Regional Commanders, are members of the admissions department staff who oversee all candidates from their part of the country. Each region also has a Diversity Officer, and there are specialists in admissions for recruited athletes and other categories, just as with West Point.

Your Blue and Gold Officer will also conduct your official interview when you reach that part of the process.

Candidate Information System

If your preliminary application is strong enough, you will be invited to complete the full online application. Structurally, it's similar to the West Point system (though each academy handles its own IT), with a list of requirements and a notification whether you have or have not completed each step.

You will need to submit two, rather than three, teacher evaluations: one from a math teacher and one from an English teacher, and both teachers should be from the current or previous academic year. In most cases, this will mean your eleventh grade teachers. Remember that teachers are asked to write a large number of recommendations each year; get your name in early. You will enter the teachers' names and email addresses in the system, and they will receive an email with instructions. Follow up to be sure that the emails don't end up in a spam folder.

SPECIAL NOTE! There have been cases when a particular teacher disapproves of the military enough to refuse to evaluate you for an academy appointment or allows personal feelings to affect the evaluation. This is unlikely, but it has happened. Because you are more restricted in your choice of teacher evaluations at the Naval Academy, this can pose a real problem. Contact your Blue and Gold Officer to explain the situation and follow his or her guidance.

You can submit additional letters if you want to, but make sure those letters address important aspects of leadership, academic, or athletic performance, and provide information that the academy's admissions office won't otherwise know about.

If you are also applying for an NROTC scholarship, you can use the same recommendations for each, but they'll have to be uploaded separately to the two different systems.

A TALE OF TWO REFERENCES! Back in my days as a career counselor, I once had a client fresh out of college who listed the President's National Security Advisor as a reference. I asked how he knew the National Security Advisor, and it turned out his father knew him. I recommended against using that person as a reference, even though it was a very prestigious person, because the National Security Advisor had no personal knowledge of my client's abilities. It was just name-dropping.

Another client listed the singer Aretha Franklin as a reference. In this case, it turned out the client had been Aretha's babysitter when she was in high school. While you wouldn't normally list babysitting experience on a college (or job) application, in this case, I recommended an exception. Aretha actually knew her well enough to say something meaningful and specific—and the name-dropping was just a bonus.

If you know somebody important, it's always tempting to get his or her name into your application file, but beware. Unless that person actually knows you well enough to say something specific and meaningful, it's more likely to backfire than to help.

Reapplying

If you don't get in on your first try and reapply the following year, you'll need to submit new recommendations (you'll have new "current year" teachers) and new personal statements.

COAST GUARD ACADEMY

The Coast Guard Academy accepts applications beginning in August for the class starting in the summer of the following year. Unlike all the other academies, you don't require a nomination to get in, so that part of the process doesn't apply. Also unlike the other academies, the Coast Guard has an Early Action option. If you pursue Early Action, your deadline for completing all forms is October 15; otherwise it's January 15.

At the Coast Guard Academy, your liaison officer is known as an Academy Admissions Partner. They operate the same way as Field Force Representatives and Blue and Gold Officers.

You will arrange for teacher evaluations from your guidance counselor, your English teacher, and your math teacher. If you're applying to more than one academy, you can use the same teachers. You may also submit additional letters of recommendation, but make sure they're substantial.

Unlike the other academies, the Coast Guard Academy requires that you have no financial debt. If you are applying as a transfer student and you have outstanding college loans, you must either pay them off, get the lending institution to defer the loans until after graduation, or transfer them to a parent or guardian in order to be eligible to apply. Even an outstanding car loan will make you ineligible, so make sure every financial obligation you have is resolved before you apply.

As part of the application process, you will need to provide a résumé along with the other items. One other notable difference is that the Coast Guard uses the Physical Fitness Examination (PFE) instead of the Candidate Fitness Assessment (CFA) used by the other academies. The PFE will be readministered during the first week of Swab Summer, the Coast Guard's equivalent of cadet basic training, and if you fail to meet the minimum score, you will be disenrolled, so keep exercising!

SPECIAL NOTE! The Coast Guard Academy will accept CFA scores in lieu of PFE scores, but they "strongly recommend" you take the PFE. If you have to take the CFA for other academies, it's tempting to drop the other test, but you shouldn't unless you have a compelling reason. In general, you should assume that "strongly recommended" is pretty much the same as "do it."

MERCHANT MARINE ACADEMY

The applications process begins on May 15 of the year prior to the year you wish to enter the Merchant Marine Academy and the deadline is March 1 of the following year. However, you don't have to wait to get yourself organized, because unique among the academies, the Merchant Marine Academy's application is available as a PDF download as well as online. Apply whichever way you like, but definitely download a copy as a tool to get yourself organized.

The application is in three parts. Parts 1 and 2 are completed by you, the candidate. Part 3 (if you use the paper version) is completed by your high school—all you fill in is your name and Social Security number.

Application Process

In the first part of the application, you'll provide standard basic data, such as name, address, Social Security number, and answer some "Yes" or "No" questions. The paper form is designed to be machine readable, so you'll fill in circles for every item. This section doesn't require any writing.

The second part focuses on athletics and extracurricular experiences. You can attach a résumé in lieu of filling out the form. As part of this section, you will write a biographical sketch of at least two hundred words explaining why you want to go to the academy, what you want to study, how you developed your career interests, and whether you have any sailing experience. As part of the essay, you must state that you understand and are willing to fulfill your service obligation after graduation. (Remember that the Merchant Marine service obligation is somewhat different from the other academies, as explained in chapter 1 and laid out officially in appendix I.)

After filling out your name and Social Security number on part III, you'll take that to your school's guidance office, who will supply an official transcript, a school profile, test scores, and class rank. (If your school doesn't provide class rank, they are asked to provide an approximation instead.)

The Merchant Marine Academy wants at least three letters of recommendation, one from the school official completing the form (typically your guidance counselor) and at least two others. Unlike the other academies, these additional letters can come from school administrators, teachers of any subject, or coaches, as long as they know you well. If you're applying to other academies, you can have the same people submit their letters to the Merchant Marine Academy as well. If you submit additional letters, they should illuminate some part of your character, qualifications, or aptitude in a way that the basic recommendations do not.

If you're applying on paper, you will assemble all three parts of the application and send them in together. If you're applying online, you'll arrange to upload the necessary additional documents.

Local Admissions Field Reps

The Merchant Marine Academy liaison officers are known as Local Admissions Field Reps. You can find a list of them on the website at www.usmma.edu/admissions/local-admissions-field-reps.

AIR FORCE ACADEMY

The Air Force Academy's admissions website (www.academyadmissions.com) is different from the website for the academy as a whole (www.usafa.af.mil). You should visit both sites as part of familiarizing yourself with the academy and its programs. As befits the high technology world of the Air Force, their iPhone and Android app is (at the time of writing) the only one that allows you access to your candidate portal.

Unless you are applying to Summer Seminar, the earliest date you can begin your application is March 1 of your junior year in high school. All applications must be complete by December 31 of that year. As with the other academies, the first step is to complete a Pre-Candidate Questionnaire; if your initial application is deemed competitive, you'll have the opportunity to complete the entire application.

Summer Seminar

The Air Force Academy's program for high school juniors is known as Summer Seminar, and the application form can be found here: www.academyadmissions.com/admissions/outreach-programs/summer-seminar/.

Your Summer Seminar application doesn't automatically turn into a Preliminary Application, as is the case with West Point and the Naval Academy. However, if you already have PSAT, PLAN, ACT, or SAT scores at the time you apply for Summer Seminar, you can opt to have your Summer Seminar application serve both purposes. If you don't have any test scores at the time you apply for Summer Seminar, you can't go back and add them.

Summer Seminar applications open on December 1 and end on January 31 each year; you'll receive an email letting you know whether you were chosen by March 6.

Academy Liaison Officer

At the Air Force Academy, your liaison officer is known as an ALO (Academy Liaison Officer). You'll see a link at the top of the admissions homepage labeled "Find your ALO." As always, your ALO is a great resource. You can reach out to your ALO even before you start the process to answer questions or get advice.

While you're searching for your ALO, be sure to check for information on outreach and diversity events in your area, located on the same search page.

Teacher Evaluations and Letters of Recommendation

The Air Force Academy requires three teacher evaluations, all from eleventh or twelfth grade instructors. One evaluation must come from an English teacher, one from a math teacher, and the third a teacher of any other subject. They prefer a science teacher, but will accept others.

In addition, the Air Force Academy "strongly encourages" you to submit up to (but no more than) three letters of recommendation from other people. These letters should be from people who know you well, and should focus on your character, integrity, leadership ability, and life experiences.

SPECIAL NOTE! Whenever you ask people for a reference or a letter of recommendation, understand that they may not remember everything about you, or necessarily know what the evaluator on the other end is looking for. It's up to you to prepare them to do a great job. Give them information on the school or other institution, and let them know what factors you think are likely to be most important. Prepare a résumé or information sheet about yourself. Identify any particular areas you think the letter should focus on. Be available to answer questions.

This advice is not only relevant when applying for an academy appointment, but will be true when you enter the job market as well.

Personal Data Record and Drug and Alcohol Abuse Certificate

There are two special forms for Air Force Academy applicants that are a bit different from the other academies: the Personal Data Record (USAFA Form 146) and the Drug and Alcohol Abuse Certificate. While you'll need to supply the same information eventually to all the academies, the timing and format is different.

You can download a copy of the Personal Data Record for early review here (the official version will be part of your candidate portal): www.reginfo.gov/public/do/DownloadDocument?documentID=37626 &version=1. Note in particular the section on encounters with law enforcement. Post-acceptance, you'll be required to get a certificate from the police or court system detailing any criminal record to confirm.

All the academies will want to know about any history of drug or alcohol abuse. Usually, you'll answer questions as part of the medical evaluation process (DoDMERB), covered in chapter 7. The Air Force Academy requires that you complete the Drug and Alcohol Abuse Certificate (AF Form 2030) as part of your application. Your ALO will go over the form with you in person to make sure you understand it fully before you are asked to sign.

While your online portal won't show you the form until you've reached that stage of the process, AF Form 2030 can easily be found online various places, including here: www.idaho.ang.af.mil/shared/media/document/AFD-120925-040.pdf.

Minor experimental use of marijuana isn't disqualifying, as the form makes clear. Lying about it, however, is. Once you sign your AF Form 2030, however, any use of marijuana, underage use of alcohol, or other drug abuse will cause any offer of admission to be withdrawn. You'll be asked to recertify your answers on a new paper copy of AF Form 2030 on your arrival at the academy, as well as undergo a drug test. (There's also a drug test administered as part of the medical exam.)

Once you're ready, start your online application to the Air Force Academy here: https://admissions.usafa.edu/gateway/Register.aspx.

HOW YOU ARE EVALUATED

Behind the scenes, each academy's admission department is hard at work sorting through thousands of candidate applications and ranking them in order of merit. While the exact scoring algorithm is a secret, the overall process is not. You are evaluated on a "whole person" concept, based 60 percent on academic achievement, 30 percent on leadership potential, and 10 percent on physical aptitude.

Each academy admissions team develops its own internal scoring methodology. In one academy's case, the system works like this. You can receive up to 800 points in each of the following categories:

- Academics
- Class Rank
- Physical and Sports Leadership
- Extracurricular Activities
- Community Influence
- Recommendations
- Candidate Fitness Assessment

Most of the categories have subcategories as well. They are weighted differently according to a complex algorithm known only to the admissions department that parallels the 60/30/10 breakdown above. The final score is expressed on the same scale, a number between 1 and 800.

Only about 150 students of the 1,200 or so admitted had consolidated scores of 700 or above. Eighty percent of the admitted class had scores between 550 and 699. This means that a few candidates were accepted with scores under 550. These candidates probably had some outstanding merit in another area, enough to compensate for weaknesses elsewhere. Most often, such weaknesses are in the area of academic preparation, so the majority of these candidates are offered appointments to the Prep School instead of the main academy.

SPECIAL NOTE! You can add information to your file up until the closing date. If you have already finished a section but suddenly win an award or achieve a distinction, go back and add the information. If for some reason the system won't let you, contact your academy liaison officer or regional commander for help. Note that you will normally need to provide contact information to confirm the new information.

Academics and Class Rank

Academics make up 60 percent of your evaluation, but notice that in the more detailed breakdown there are two categories: academics and class rank. Your academics score includes standardized test reports, grade point average (be sure to specify whether your GPA is weighted or unweighted), and whether you've taken all the required or recommended courses.

Class rank, you'll note, is a separate category. The academies place substantial weight on your class rank, because they always want to know how you stack up against your peer group. Class rank also helps compensate for the reality that some high schools are more academically challenging than others.

Many high schools do not provide class rankings. If yours doesn't, you'll indicate that fact on your application (usually by entering "1" for rank and "1" for class size). The academies will get in touch with your guidance counselor to find out your approximate level. The Air Force Academy generally requires its candidates to be in the top 40 percent of their class, but in practice most members of their incoming classes rank in the top 3 percent.[1]

If you're homeschooled, class rank is often not applicable. As discussed in chapter 6, the academies place greater weight on standardized test scores when considering homeschooled candidates.

The academies will want a school profile[2] from your guidance office. A school profile includes information on GPA and test score breakdown among students, percentage of student who go on to higher education, and any awards and honors held by the school. You can read a sample one here: https://professionals.collegeboard.com/guidance/counseling/profile/sample.

Because it's not fair to judge candidates by the quality of the high schools they attended, your level of high school achievement is considered in the context of your school profile. If your school is less challenging, you're expected to do better in comparison to your peer group. If your school is highly competitive, they'll take that into account in evaluating your accomplishments as well.

Physical and Sports Leadership

Although the CFA, as mentioned earlier, is scored pass/fail, the overall quality and extent of your athletic achievement is an important part of your total candidate score. This score includes the sports you play, awards or recognition you've received (including team awards, such as regional or state championships), along with leadership roles, such as team captain.

Community Influence

Extracurricular activities are counted separately from a measure of "community influence," which is heavily weighted toward leadership roles and other ways in which you can show that you make a difference. If you're in Scouting, for example, a number of merit badges you might pursue involve community activities to some extent. Be sure to list them as achievements separately from the acquisition of the merit badge itself.

Recommendations

You can see how important it is that you cultivate teachers and others who can write meaningfully about your accomplishments and character. A reference containing little more than glittering generalities will have less effect than one with detail and substance.

People whom you ask for references may not always know as much about you as you think they do. As a general life rule, you should always prepare your references. Let them know what it is you're trying to achieve and give them information on what the recipient is looking for: leadership, character, creative problem-solving skills, or whatever. Print out web pages and other material that may help the recommender. Prepare a résumé of your accomplishments to make it easier for the recommender to cite them.

Think about your choice of references. For certain teacher recommendations, the academies have already specified whom they want. You can always provide additional letters (not too many) if they can help illuminate your qualifications in ways not otherwise handled.

Make sure your references actually like you and think well of you! More than one candidate has inadvertently listed a reference who didn't say good things about him or her. If there's a real problem with a mandatory reference, talk with your guidance counselor or academy liaison officer about the best way to proceed.

MANAGING YOUR PORTAL

Check your portal regularly (at least weekly) throughout the process. Keep a checklist of what is and is not complete. Don't forget you are responsible for everything on the portal, even material that other people are supposed to supply. Follow up as necessary.

While you'll receive formal notice of admission through the mail, it will also appear on the portal. My son found out he'd been accepted at West Point online two days before the actual acceptance packet showed up. You'll let the academy know whether you accept the appointment through your portal.

Once you're accepted, you still aren't done with the portal. There are many things you'll need to do between getting in and reporting to the academy. We'll cover that part of the process in chapter 8.

In the meantime, you need to get a nomination.

Getting a Nomination

UNDERSTANDING NOMINATIONS

One of the unique factors in applying to a military service academy is the need to obtain a *nomination*. Nominations are designed to ensure geographic diversity at the academies, so that the leadership of the military resembles the nation as a whole.

> **SPECIAL NOTE!** To be admitted, you need both a nomination and an appointment. The appointment comes from the academy itself. The nomination can come from a variety of sources. However, you cannot be given an appointment if you don't have a nomination.

You must have a nomination to get in! (The US Coast Guard Academy is the one exception. If you're only applying to the Coast Guard Academy, you can skip this chapter altogether.) Usually, you can apply for a nomination from at least four sources: your local congressperson, both US senators for your state, and the vice president.

Although you must have a nomination to get in, nominations aren't a guarantee of admission. The academy, not your member of Congress, makes the final decision of whom to admit. Check out the West Point class profile in Appendix II: 4,120 candidates got nominations, 2,360 were found qualified, but only 1,257 got in.

Every one of those 1,257 candidates had a nomination. However, some of the qualified candidates didn't get nominations, and even though the academy liked them, the lack of a nomination was fatal.

> **SPECIAL NOTE!** *Apply to every nomination source for which you're eligible!*

SOURCES OF NOMINATIONS

There are a number of different nomination sources for academy appointments. The Federal statutes that govern the nominations process for each academy can be found in appendix I. West Point, the Naval Academy, and the Air Force Academy all work the same way. The Merchant Marine Academy process is a little different, so it's described in a section of its own. As noted earlier, the Coast Guard Academy doesn't require nominations at all, though there are occasional attempts to change that.

> **SPECIAL NOTE!** In this chapter, the word "nomination" has two meanings. For you as an applicant, a nomination is something that you get that allows an academy to appoint you if they choose to. Legally, however, a nomination is a slot at one of the academies. Each nomination source has a certain limited number of slots available. If you're appointed and take one of those slots, you've used it up until you leave (hopefully by graduating).
>
> This can be confusing. If you're on a list of ten names submitted by your senator or congressperson, you are considered "nominated" in the first sense. In the second sense, all ten of you are candidates for a *single* nomination.

Senatorial and Congressional Nominations

Each member of Congress and each US senator is entitled to five nominations for each of the three major service academies. *That's five nominations for all classes put together, not five nominations for each class!* Normally, one (and occasionally two) nomination slots are available each year because of graduations or other departures.

Each senator and representative can nominate up to ten candidates for each vacancy. Nominators can choose to submit those names unranked, or choose one as the principal candidate, who will be selected if he or she meets the qualifications. If the nominator chooses a principal candidate, the remaining candidates can be submitted ranked or unranked. If they are ranked, the academy will consider each one in turn until one is found qualified; if unranked, the academy chooses the one it thinks is best.

You can apply for a nomination from both US senators of the state in which you reside, and from the representative of the congressional district in which you live. To find the names and addresses of your two senators, visit www.senate.gov/general/contact_information/senators_cfm.cfm and select your state. For your member of Congress, visit www.house.gov/representatives/find/ and enter your ZIP code. (In some cases, you may need to enter your ZIP+4 or street address to get an exact match, as Congressional district lines don't always line up with ZIP code boundaries.)

Once you know who your representatives are, click on the links provided to go to their official websites, and look for "Service Academy Nominations." Sometimes you'll find it under "Constituent Services," sometimes under "Student Resources," and sometimes you may have to search a little bit—there isn't an official template for these websites and each office does it differently. You'll normally find forms and instructions available for download, or at least some information on your next step.

> **SPECIAL NOTE!** Start your nomination process as early as possible. Most offices have an absolute cut-off date for applications, and if you miss them, you're out of luck until the following year. Even if you won't be able to apply until next year, it's still a good idea to check out the process and download the forms to see what is expected of you.

US Territories and Overseas Possessions

In addition to states, the United States has various territories and overseas possessions. If you live in one of these areas, your delegate in Congress or other official may have the ability to offer nominations to a service academy, as shown in table 5-1.

Table 5-1. Nominations for US Territories and Overseas Possessions

Territory	Number of Nominations	Who Nominates
District of Columbia	5	Delegate to the House of Representatives
Virgin Islands	3	Delegate in Congress
Puerto Rico	5	Resident Commissioner from Puerto Rico
Puerto Rico	1*	Governor of Puerto Rico (*nominee must be a native of Puerto Rico)
Guam	3	Delegate in Congress
American Samoa	2	Delegate in Congress
Northern Mariana Islands	2	Delegate in Congress

SPECIAL NOTE! From now on, when we refer to "members of Congress," we mean representatives, senators, and delegates, because the basic process is the same for all of them.

Like members of Congress and senators, these nominees can submit up to ten names for every vacancy. Nominators can choose to submit those names unranked, or choose one as the principal candidate, who will be selected if he or she meets the qualifications. If the nominator chooses a principal candidate, the remaining candidates can be submitted ranked or unranked.

To locate the various delegates and the resident commissioner from Puerto Rico, visit the House of Representatives site at www.house.gov/representatives/find/. The website for the governor of Puerto Rico is at www.fortaleza.pr.gov.

Vice President of the United States

Because the vice president of the United States is also president of the Senate under the Constitution, his office has five nominations, the same as any other senator. Everyone is eligible to apply for a vice presidential nomination. The exact website address changes with each administration; currently it's www.whitehouse.gov/administration/vice-president-biden/academy-nominations. (You can Google "vice president service academy nominations" if that doesn't work.)

As you can imagine, the vice president gets thousands of applications. Instead of having his office sort through and rank all the applicants, the vice president delegates the selection to the individual academies, giving the admissions office an opportunity to pick five additional worthy candidates.

While the odds of getting a vice presidential nomination are small, you should definitely apply. All you have to do is fill out a brief form saying you want to be considered. You don't have to send anything else; the academies already have the information as a product of your application.

The vice president does not have any nominations for the Merchant Marine Academy.

Presidential Nominations

The president of the United States has at least 165 nominations, broken into several categories with specific eligibility requirements.

(Again, that's for all classes for each academy; the number available in a given year will be about a fourth of the total.) Like the vice president, the president delegates the actual selection process to the academies.

If you're eligible, you'll apply for a presidential nomination directly to the academy. You will have to provide proof that you meet the requirements of the category. The academies will rank the candidates for each nomination category in order of merit, and award the nominations in that order until they're used up.

To apply, write a letter to the academy. Appendix IV contains sample letters taken from each academy's website. You will need to provide documentation for your claims. If you don't already have all the necessary records on file, start gathering them now—it tends to take longer than you think. Always submit copies, never originals.

The president does not nominate candidates for the Merchant Marine Academy, and of course no nominations are required for the Coast Guard Academy.

SPECIAL NOTE! If you search for "presidential nominations" on an academy website and come up short, you should know that the academies use their own terms for them: "Service-Connected Nomination" at West Point and "Military-Affiliated Nomination" at both the Naval and Air Force Academies.

Here are the categories and qualifications for presidential nominations.

Children of Wounded, Killed, or Missing Veterans

The president has sixty-five nominations for children of members of the armed forces who

- were killed in action;
- died of or have a service-connected disability rated at 100 percent or greater resulting from wounds or injuries received or diseases contracted during active service, or have a preexisting injury or disease aggravated by active service that resulted in death or 100 percent or greater disability; or
- are in "missing status" (this includes children of certain civilian employees. (See appendix I.)

Children of Active Duty or Retired Military

There are a hundred presidential nominations for children of members of the armed forces who have at least eight years of active duty, are retired with pay, in the reserves with at least eight years of credited service, or eligible for retirement pay except for not yet being sixty years old. If your parent died while receiving retirement pay (or eligible for retirement pay except for age), you also qualify in this category.

If you're eligible in the category of children of dead, wounded, or disabled veterans, you aren't eligible for this category—but remember that though there are fewer nominations in the first category, there are also far fewer candidates.

Children of Medal of Honor Winners

The third and final category of presidential nominations is reserved for children of Medal of Honor winners. There are unlimited nominations available in this category, but of course there are very few eligible candidates.

Current Military or Reserve Nominations

If you are already serving as an enlisted member of the armed forces or in a reserve component, you are eligible for a nomination from one of the three Service Secretaries (Army, Navy, Air Force). There are eighty-five nominations available for active duty enlisted personnel and eighty-five for members of reserve components. You must meet the basic requirements listed at the beginning of chapter 2.

The process is similar for both active and reserve. You will need a nomination from your company commander, then you will go through the admissions process just like any other candidate. You may find the section on "Advice for Late Starters" in chapter 3 of use, especially if you've been out of high school for a while.

If you need recent SAT/ACT scores, the tests (and review courses) are available in the military. Candidates for academy appointments are automatically considered for the appropriate prep school.

JROTC/ROTC Honor Units with Distinction

A total of twenty nominations are reserved for honor graduates of ROTC or JROTC programs designated as "honor units of distinction." If you qualify, your teacher or professor will begin the nominations process for you.

Nominations You Can't Apply For

As we've learned, senators and representatives are allowed to submit up to ten names for each available nomination. The person who receives the actual nomination is considered to have "won the district." That leaves nine people who were on the list, but who didn't get in. What happens to them?

If you're one of the nine, don't give up hope. You can still get in. The academies have additional nominations available to award. If you're rated as "qualified" but don't win the specific nomination slot for which you were competing, you are automatically considered for these additional categories. You don't have to take any additional steps to qualify.

There's a fairly large gap between the number of nominations we've discussed so far and the total number of cadets and midshipmen that get admitted each year, shown in table 5-2.

Table 5-2. Nominations Available from All Sources

Category	Number of Nominators	Total Number of Nominations	Per Class (Actual number varies slightly from year to year)
Senators	100	500	125
Representatives in Congress	435	2175	540
US Territories/Possessions	7	21	5
Vice President	1	5	1
President (does not include children of Medal of Honor winners)	1	165	40
Current Enlisted	1	170	40
ROTC/JROTC Honor Schools	20	20	5
Service Secretary	1	150	35
Superintendent	1	50	50
TOTAL	**567**	**3256**	**841**

The authorized strength of the three major academies is 4,400. (Based on appropriations in a particular year, actual attendance may be higher or lower.) Subtract out the 3,256 from the table, and you're left with 1,144 people, or somewhere between 285 and 290 for each incoming class.

Those additional nomination slots are awarded in order of merit to candidates rated "qualified" but who didn't win the primary nomination for which they were competing. If you're high enough on that list of "qualified alternates," you'll get an offer.

If you're selected in this way, your slot isn't charged to your state or Congressional district; it comes off a different list. (By the way, if this happens to you, you won't necessarily know it; it will still look as if you're getting the nomination from your senator or congressperson.)

Here are the remaining categories of nominations.

Service Secretary Nominations for Qualified Alternates

The Service Secretary (Secretary of the Army, Secretary of the Navy, Secretary of the Air Force) has 150 nominations available for qualified alternates, awarded in order of merit. In practice, the academy admissions office makes the decisions.

Superintendent's Nominations

The superintendent of each academy has fifty nominations available each year. These are often used for recruited athletes, but may be used for other purposes. Last year, West Point awarded only twenty nominations in this category, suggesting that they prefer to use other nomination sources when they can.

Remaining Vacancy Nominations

For the remaining vacancies, the Service Secretary (again, in practice, the academy admissions department) nominates as many cadets or midshipmen as necessary to bring the class to full strength. These are drawn from the same list of qualified alternates in the order of merit. At least three-quarters of cadets and midshipmen selected under this category must be from people who were on various congressional lists but not chosen under that category.

National Waiting List

What if you *still* don't get in? As with all colleges and universities, some people who are offered admission to a service academy choose something else instead. At the Merchant Marine Academy for the Class of 2018 (they're the only one that reported this information), 378 candidates were offered appointments, but the final class size was 252. Whenever someone decides not to attend, that slot becomes available again, and goes to the next person on the list. There are cases in which people have found out only weeks before reporting day that they have been selected to attend.

INTERNATIONAL CADETS

As specified in the academy laws (appendix I), a certain number of foreign students are admitted to US military service academies each year. The purpose of this program is to build better military relationship with countries important to US foreign policy. Both the number of appointments (up to sixty total) and the countries from which these cadets will be drawn are determined each year by the Department of Defense.

These appointments are outside normal channels and they do not count toward the total size of the incoming class. The foreign countries in question are required to reimburse the academy for the cost, and people admitted under this program do not have a responsibility to serve in the US military, though most go on to perform military service in their own countries. Applicants must meet normal qualification standards.

If you're in this category, begin the process by contacting the US Defense Attaché's office at the American Embassy in your home country. Typically, you will need to be sponsored by a national-level government official, and each nation can nominate up to six candidates. Unlike other candidates, the age cutoff for people in this category is twenty-two.

If you're an American citizen who wants to study at another nation's military academy, contact the defense attaché for the appropriate country. Each year, a certain number of American service academy cadets study abroad as part of their education; those opportunities are handled by the academies themselves.

MERCHANT MARINE ACADEMY NOMINATIONS

As noted earlier, the nominations system for the Merchant Marine Academy is slightly different.

Congressional nominations. Instead of five nominations per senator and five nominations per member of Congress, the nominations are apportioned by state in proportion to their congressional representation. If your state has five members of Congress, the two senators and five representatives are all nominating candidates for the same five nomination slots.

Territories and Possessions. US territories and possessions have fewer nominations available. The District of Columbia gets four; the

Virgin Islands, Guam, American Samoa, Puerto Rico (Resident Commissioner), and Northern Mariana Islands get one each.

In addition, the Panama Canal Commission has two nominations for people who qualify under certain treaties and regulations, set out in the Merchant Marine Academy regulations in appendix I, section (b) (5). If you're a resident of Panama or a dependent of a US government employee working for the Panama Canal Zone, and think you qualify, visit www.pancanal.com or contact the Merchant Marine Academy directly for information.

As with the other three academies that require nominations, all remaining positions are filled in order of merit from qualified alternates.

DO I NEED TO BRIBE MY CONGRESSPERSON?

As soon as the word got out about our son's ambition, people started suggesting to us that we needed to donate to our congressman, volunteer on his campaign, and otherwise use any and all political influence we could muster if we wanted to give our son a fighting chance.

This is, I'm happy to say, nonsense. You don't have to do anything of the sort, and if you do, it's just as likely to backfire as to help. Your credentials, not your connections, determine whether you get a nomination.

What makes us so sure? In 2014, *USA Today* ran an article about political appointments to service academies.[1] In it, they note that at least some nominations go to children of friends, political supporters, and donors to the lawmakers' campaigns. The article points out some of the flaws in the congressional nominations process: the system isn't particularly transparent, there are no universal standard or ethical guidelines, and the process is certainly not consistent among the 535 nominators. While the congressional nomination system provides for geographic diversity, it doesn't do much for other kinds of diversity.

These things are true, but they aren't the whole story. The article doesn't cite any specific cases of abuse, but merely warns of the potential dangers—and if they'd found actual abuses, they would certainly have published them. That strongly suggests that the role of political influence in Congressional nominations is pretty low, if not nonexistent.

There's a very good reason for this: a nomination doesn't get somebody an appointment. If a member of Congress chose to nominate Mr. and Mrs. Rich Donor's unqualified child for an academy appointment, the kid would most likely be rejected by the academy—and the Donor family isn't likely to be happy about it. If the Donor child is actually highly qualified, then he or she deserves to be considered just like anybody else. It's much better for the members of Congress to run an open, fair, and competitive process.

That's why most congressional and senatorial offices appoint a volunteer advisory board, usually consisting of active duty or retired military officers and notable civilians, to evaluate applicants and recommend a slate of candidates. A staffer in the member's office usually administers the process. Occasionally, a member of Congress may personally interview some of the finalists, but this is uncommon.

So if you want to make a political contribution to your member of Congress or work on his or her reelection campaign, go right ahead. But don't do it just because you think it's going to help your child's chances.

SPECIAL NOTE! If you aren't well qualified, it won't matter if you're well connected.

Does that mean there are no political considerations in the process? Well, not exactly. State delegations tend to want to maximize the number of cadets and midshipmen for their states, and so there's a certain amount of horse trading that goes on. In our son's case, he received a nomination from one of our senators, and received letters from the other senator and our representative saying that while he was on their list of finalists as well, they were nominating someone else so that the maximum number of candidates had a shot at admission. (If my son had been applying to more than one academy, however, he might have received a nomination to a different academy from one of the other nominators.)

As we learned earlier, members of Congress may submit their names ranked or unranked, and with or without a principal nominee. In a follow-up to the *USA Today* article[2], only two lawmakers in the Cincinnati, Ohio, area used the "principal nominee" approach. Remember, if there's a principal nominee who is qualified, that person *must* be selected.

What's the reason? According to the representatives interviewed, when a nominee is a "slam-dunk" candidate, they will sometimes label another qualified candidate as "principal nominee." The academy must accept the principal nominee and will find another way to admit the "slam dunk" candidate.

Said the representative in question, "The appointment process for each of the military academies is extremely competitive, and my goal is to help as many deserving students from [my district] as possible attend the academy of their choice."

HOW THE CONGRESSIONAL NOMINATIONS PROCESS WORKS

Although each office develops its own system (and its own set of applications forms) for academy nominations, they tend to follow the same general format.

Administration

You'll normally find information about service academy nominations on the member's website under the category "Constituent Services." Constituent services cover a wide range of issues, from helping people with issues with federal agencies to awarding special tickets for a daily White House tour. While a member of Congress may occasionally provide some assistance personally, it's more typical that staffers do the daily work. One of those constituent service jobs is overseeing the academy nominations process.

Members of Congress have offices in Washington, DC, but they also have an office located in their district. Service academy nominations are normally handled at the district level rather than in Washington, and that is the most likely place you will find the appropriate staffer. Make sure you send correspondence and applications to the right office; the information will be in your applications package.

Administering this process is a bigger job than it may seem, and the people involved usually have other duties besides this. By all means ask when you have questions or need assistance, but don't bother them unnecessarily. (If you have any issues, don't try to contact the member of Congress directly. Instead, contact the appropriate staffer directly, either by email or phone.) Pay attention to deadlines and technical procedures. They have to organize all the information on all the candidates, so they need you to do it on time (preferably early) and according to their format. If you don't, you may not be considered at all.

SPECIAL NOTE! The final deadline given in the applications packet is usually unbreakable. If you don't make it on time, you won't be considered that year. Aim to be early so that if you have any problems, you have time to resolve them.

Informational Meeting

Some congressional offices conduct an informational meeting for people interested in service academy nominations, and often the academies will send their local liaison officers as well. If that's the case in your district, we strongly advise you to attend if at all possible. We thought ours was very worthwhile; in fact, we went again the following year.

In our case, the room was set up with tables for each academy, staffed by liaison officers, with various handouts available. In the formal program, we got a welcome from our representative, a description of the nominations process from the staffer in charge, and then an individual presentation from each academy on how their process worked. Our senators each sent their staffer in charge to describe their process. There was ample opportunity to ask questions, and afterward there was the opportunity for more one-on-one discussion.

If there's an information session, details will normally be included in the application material you download from the congressional website.

Academy Review Board

As we've mentioned, most members of Congress use outside boards to screen, review, and select candidates for nominations. People who serve on these boards are volunteers, generally from residents of the state or congressional district. Many are current or former military officers; some are themselves academy graduates.

The staffer prepares packages for each candidate and the academy review board then studies the packages and does a preliminary ranking. Incomplete or obviously noncompetitive applications normally get rejected at that point. If you're competitive, you will be called in for an interview, and depending on how the interview goes, you may move up or down on the list.

At the end, the board submits names to the member of Congress, either ranked or unranked, and either with or without a recommendation for a principal nominee. Occasionally the member of Congress will personally interview some of the finalists, but more commonly the recommendation of the board is accepted as the final nomination list. You'll get a letter signed (or robo-signed) by your representative no matter what the outcome.

The Application

Each individual office has a unique application. If you apply to your member of Congress and both senators, that's three separate applications you must complete, and each of them is different.

Part of each application duplicates material you've already provided to the academy: personal information, letters of recommendation (you usually have more latitude with these letters than with the recommendations required by the academies), lists of extracurricular activities and honors, and so on.

Some offices want you to provide a notarized affidavit of residence to certify that you are in fact a resident of the state and district. Several ask for a passport-sized photo. School photos are okay if not too informal. We heard about one kid who wanted to impress the board with his fighting spirit so had his picture taken wearing camouflage while clenching a knife between his teeth. Don't do that, or anything similar.

Most require an essay of some sort, most often on "Why I Want to Go to a Military Service Academy." Some require more than one essay. One required *eighteen*, although they were mercifully short. (We'll talk about essays next.)

All the applications contain instructions for other information they want sent. You will need to arrange with your school to send official transcripts. You will need to arrange for letters of reference. Sometimes you'll get sealed letters that you'll enclose with your package; other times your letter writers will have to send the letters themselves. Each member of Congress has code numbers to receive SAT and ACT scores; you will need to arrange with the testing companies to have your scores sent in.

> **SPECIAL NOTE!** *You*, not your school or letter writers, are responsible for making sure all the necessary material is sent to the congressional office on time. Start early and check to make sure everything went out. If they have time, your congressional office will usually warn you if some pieces of your application are not yet in, but ultimately the responsibility is yours, not anybody else's.

Personal Essays

It's very hard for most people to write good personal essays, and in some ways it's harder for a teenager. If you haven't had a great deal of life experience, if you are uncertain about some of your decisions and choices, you may have no idea how to begin an essay on "Why I

Want to Go to an Academy." The temptation is to go for maximum platitudes and steer away from anything that could possibly raise a question. A lot of your competitors will end up doing it that way.

Think of it, though, from the point of view of those doing the interviewing. As we've learned, one of the major factors in whether you'll do well at an academy is whether you really want to be there, and whether you really understand your own choice. They want to see that you've thought it through. Sometimes that means sharing some of your worries, and what you've done to overcome them.

Something else to remember about board members is that they have to read a hundred or more of these essays. They aren't going to spend ten minutes parsing your sentence to get out all the hidden meanings. Follow the "KISS" (Keep it simple, stupid!) approach: prefer the shorter to the longer, the simpler to the more complex, and the active to the passive. (And don't forget to poorfead check your spelling and grammar!) If your word processor can calculate a readability index (most can), keep it in the sixth- to eighth-grade range to make it easy and quick to read and understand. Your audience will appreciate it.

In chapter 2, we focused on your decision to pursue an academy appointment. If you did your homework in that chapter, you know why you want to go, and it's going to be a lot easier to put it down on paper.

Focus on substance, not on style. Say what you have to say clearly. Stay within word count limits. Get feedback, but remember the final choice of what to say and how to say it must be yours.

Your counselor at school may have references and information on how to write a good college essay; some junior and senior English classes include college essays among their writing topics. Most college application guides have essay guidelines and suggestions you may find of value.

We've listed some guidelines for writing college essays in appendix III.

The Interview

For most people, the interview is the most nerve-wracking part of the process. After all, you're sitting in front of a group of adults who are going to make an important decision about your future. It's silly to say you shouldn't worry, but it is a good idea to put it into perspective.

First, everybody else is guaranteed to be nervous, too. They're sweating this just like you are. Second, the interviewers understand what you're going through. (That doesn't necessarily mean they'll cut you a break, though.) Third, they've already read your file. No matter what, the interview will play a limited role in deciding whether you get the nomination.

The best way to handle the interview is to be well prepared, and that means *practice*. Recruit your own review board to interview you, and tell them not to go easy on you. If you mess up during practice, well, that's the point of practice. It doesn't count. Once you've been on the hot seat a few times, you'll get more comfortable, and there's a good chance you'll find the actual interview a lot less challenging than the practice sessions.

My son had three interviews (two senatorial and one congressional) and was on the finalist list for all three. (As mentioned, he got only one nomination officially.) In each case, he arrived, checked in, and sat with others waiting for their interviews. The interviews were very different in style and substance.

His first interview lasted about ten minutes and focused almost exclusively on whether his EMT service meant he wanted to go to medical school. (A few academy graduates do go on to medical school, but in general academies don't exist to train future doctors.) Clearly, that was the big question the board had; the application must have answered the rest.

The second interview was very short, about five minutes, with no tough questions at all, while other interviews were taking closer to twenty minutes. He came home convinced he wasn't going to get that nomination. Instead, it appears as if they made up their minds based on the application. The only thing he needed to do was not mess it up.

The third was filled with tougher questions and was overall most stressful. Some of the questions were definitely curveballs: What did he think about the morality of killing people? What was his opinion of our foreign policy in the Middle East? He assumed the goal of these questions was to see how easily he could be rattled and that his answers mattered less than how he responded.

However, we'd practiced fielding tough questions, so he had some preparation. Remember also that people do know you're still young, and you're not expected to have completely developed answers to moral questions that have plagued philosophers for millennia. Instead, if you're articulate, clear, and not too intimidated, you should do fine.

We've provided some resources on interviewing skills in appendix III.

Table 5-3 has a list of questions culled from various congressional applications that are representative of the kinds of questions you may

SPECIAL NOTE! There is no way you can be prepared for every possible question, so you need to think about what you're going to do if you get surprised. Understand that the specific answer you give is often less important than how you handle yourself. Don't be afraid to think before you speak (almost always a good idea anyway). Remember that occasionally "I don't know" can be a good answer.

When you're arranging for some practice interviews, ask your interviewers to think of some curveballs of their own. Once you've handled a few in practice, you'll be ready for the real thing.

be asked. Think about how you'd answer them. Try your answers out on a few people. Write key points on notecards; they'll help you keep yourself organized when you talk. (You can't take notecards into the interview, of course, but you can sit in your car and review them one last time before you go in.)

Table 5-3. Potential Interview Questions

1. Describe a situation in which you successfully exercised leadership. What lessons did you learn? (**TIP!** The lessons are the part they are most interested in.)
2. Describe a situation in which your leadership was lacking or resulted in a failure. What lessons did you learn? (**TIP!** Don't be afraid to explain how you messed up; everybody does. Instead, focus on what you learned and explain what you have done differently since.)
3. What is your greatest strength? Why? (**TIP!** To avoid sounding like a braggart, decide in advance what that strength is and have a couple of examples on hand.)
4. What is your greatest weakness? What are you doing to address it? (**TIP!** Don't give one of those fake answers: "My greatest weakness is that I care too much and try too hard." Everybody's got weaknesses. The key in answering this question is explaining what you are doing about it. "My biggest weakness is procrastination. I'm trying to overcome that by setting aside time each afternoon to work on some things I've been putting off.")
5. How do you know you are prepared for the rigors and demands of academy life? (**TIP!** Nobody likes everything about academy life. The question isn't how you'll cope with the parts you like or find rewarding; the question is how you'll cope with the parts you don't like at all.)
6. Do you intend to make military service a career? Why or why not? (**TIP!** Don't feel that "yes" is the only acceptable answer. If you answer "no," be prepared to explain what you plan to do after you finish your military service and why the academy is still the best place for you to be. You can also answer that you don't know or haven't decided yet.)
7. Tell us something about yourself. (**TIP!** People are often caught unawares by this question, even though it's quite common. Be prepared with an answer, and keep it under a minute. Remember that they've read your application package already. Is there something you want to highlight? Is there an overall summary you'd like them to hear? Is there something interesting about you that didn't fit on the application?)
8. Do you have any questions for us? (**TIP!** You can actually ask questions if you have them. Don't feel that you must have a question ready, but do look as if you've thought about it. Also, ask this question in reverse. "Do you have any other questions for me?")

Be prepared to answer all of these in a short, clear way, and you should be able to handle anything the board throws at you. Look over your application. Does it raise any specific questions? If so, practice answering those as well.

Dress professionally, as if for a job interview. For men, a suit is certainly appropriate, but a blazer, slacks, and tie is acceptable. Women have a wider range of options, but have the same goal. Some JROTC/ROTC members wear their uniforms; that's up to you. Be well groomed. A recent haircut, shined shoes, and trimmed fingernails are always appropriate.

Decision

There's a deadline for congressional offices to send in their list of nominations, and once they're official, letters get sent out informing everyone of the decision.

Check your admissions portal regularly. In our son's case, he learned he'd gotten a nomination by checking his file; the actual letter came two days later. Be sure to verify that the nomination has actually shown up on your candidate portal.

6

Special Issues and Concerns

You may have individual issues, concerns, or questions that don't necessarily apply to the candidate population as a whole.

The major academies (West Point, Navy, Air Force) compete in a variety of NCAA Division I sports; the smaller (Coast Guard and Merchant Marine) compete in Division III. Like other colleges and universities, they recruit athletes. Perhaps you want to be one of them.

Historically, some groups have been either denied admission or have seen their opportunities restricted. If you're a woman, a minority, LGBT (lesbian, gay, bisexual, or transgender), or are part of a less common religion (or none at all), what are the current policies? Are there issues or circumstances you need to know about before you go?

What if you haven't had the range of opportunities of other candidates because of your economic status or the school you attend? What if you've experienced unusual hardships or life challenges?

What if you've been homeschooled or have otherwise had a non-traditional education? The applications process is set up for people who attended a public or private high school, but homeschooled students are considered on an equal basis. You'll have to do a few special things, however, to make sure the academies have enough information to evaluate you properly.

Some people have had trouble in their backgrounds. Were you suspended in high school? Have you had encounters with law enforcement? Did you ever smoke or drink something you shouldn't have? You're not necessarily out of the running as far as an academy appointment is concerned, but you're going to have to face the issue directly and honestly.

While you must be a US citizen to attend an academy (except for a few foreign exchange students, as discussed in chapter 5), you may be in the process of getting your citizenship or you may have dual citizenship. How do you address these issues in pursuing an academy appointment?

Of course, there are many other possible concerns or issues that may apply to you. If yours isn't covered in this chapter, first talk with your school guidance counselor and then with your academy liaison officer.

RECRUITED ATHLETES

Playing sports for an academy isn't exactly the same as playing for a regular college or university. First, there's no extra financial benefit. You get a 100 percent scholarship whether or not you play. Second, there are no special easy classes for academically challenged athletes. You'll have to keep up with the same course load as everybody else. Third, it's not a good route to the pros, if that's your goal. You've got a five-year service obligation to fulfill. (In rare cases, you may be allowed to turn pro after two years, but these exceptions are few and far between.)

On the plus side, being a recruited athlete can be a great way to get admitted to an academy. As long as you're rated as qualified, even if you don't "win your district," you can get in. If your academics aren't as strong as your athletics, note that some prep school slots are reserved for athletes who need the extra academic preparation. While the academies won't give you a break on course load, they will work to make sure you have the tools you need.

If you're a star athlete, the academies may be among the colleges and universities that seek you out. There are some people who never thought about attending a service academy until approached by a recruiter. (Under NCAA rules, only certain people are allowed to recruit for college sports. If you're in doubt as to the situation or the person you're speaking to, ask directly: "Am I being recruited?")

You don't have to leave being recruited to chance, however. If you are competitive at Division I levels for a particular sport (or III for Coast Guard and Merchant Marine), and you want to go to an academy, you can approach the athletic department directly and try to get them interested in you.

Gene McIntyre, West Point's Director of Admissions Support and Associate Athletic Director, gave some point-by-point guidance on the topic. His bottom-line advice? "Make it easy for your recruiter."

Getting Started

The first thing you should do is to sit down and have a candid discussion with your high school coach about whether you're Division I (or III) material. A good time to have that conversation is in the spring of your sophomore year and definitely not too far into your junior year. If you need to get your game up, you've still got time. If you're not competitive at that level, then you can still pursue an academy appointment just like anybody else.

Your coach has information on websites that host highlight videos of athletes for recruiters to view. If at all possible, have a video of your performance uploaded to that site.

Next, consult the list of websites in table 6-1 to find the particular coach for the academy and sport you want.

Table 6-1. Academy Athletic Department Contacts

Academy	Website
West Point	www.goarmysports.com/recruiting/recruiting-questionnaires.html
Naval Academy	www.navysports.com/recruiting/navy-recruiting.html
Coast Guard Academy	www.uscgasports.com/information/directory/index
Merchant Marine Academy	www.usmmasports.com/information/directory/index
Air Force Academy	www.goairforcefalcons.com/compliance/afa-recruits.html#

If there's an online application or questionnaire, complete it. In addition, send a short email to the head coach of the sport introducing yourself and stating your desire to attend. Make sure your email includes the following:

- Your contact information
- The contact information for your high school head coach
- Vitals: height, weight, position played
- Brief summary of sports record; link to your video

If you have already opened your application file at the academy, tell them that, too. If you would be willing to attend the prep school, say so specifically. That can be an important factor.

Managing the Process

Remember that coaches have to review a large number of prospects, but they will reach out if they are interested in you. You should generally expect to hear back from the coach in a couple of weeks; if you haven't heard anything, follow up after about three weeks. In the meantime, continue your applications process and quest for a nomination.

If the coach is interested in you, the athletic department will work with admissions to help you through the process. *Keep in regular touch with your coach!* (That means *you*, not your parents. If the coach hears from your parents more often than from you, it raises real questions about your actual desire to attend an academy.)

Send transcripts and test scores to the coach in the spring of your junior year in addition to making sure they're uploaded to your applications portal. (You can send informal copies to the coach as long as the official copies go to admissions.)

> **SPECIAL NOTE!** You may hear the rumor that recruited athletes get superintendent nominations, but that's not automatic by any means. Athletes should apply for every nomination they can, just like any other candidate. Superintendent nominations are only used for special cases and emergencies, and you should never count on getting one.

Physical Qualifications and Health Issues

In chapter 7, we'll discuss the Candidate Fitness Assessment (CFA) and the medical clearance process, known as DoDMERB, in detail. There are, however, a few special issues that apply to recruited athletes.

First, it's strongly recommended that you take the CFA during the summer—or at least not during your athletic season, when you'll be tired and may be hurt.

Second, start the medical clearance process as early as possible. You'll get information about scheduling the examination. As you'll see, problems getting medical clearance are pretty common, and they take time to clear up. Your prospective coach will probably want to ask if you have any of the following issues: ADHD/mood disorders, asthma/inhaler use, surgery, concussions, vision not correctable to 20/20, or color blindness. He or she may also ask about any medications you take regularly.

If you have these issues, they won't automatically or necessarily keep you out of an academy, but they will at least trigger requests for additional information and tests, which take time to resolve. That's a good reason to get out in front of any such issues as quickly as possible.

Again, keep your prospective coach informed of your progress through the medical clearance process.

ECONOMICALLY DISADVANTAGED/HARDSHIP CANDIDATES

In *The Long Gray Line*, Rick Atkinson's story of the West Point Class of 1966, he recounts this story.[1] "Once, when he was a little boy, Tom had ridden a train with his mother and aunt to his grandmother's house in upstate New York. Suddenly he spied an immense fortress of gray stone across the Hudson. 'Look, Tommy,' his mother said, 'that's West Point up there. That's a school for soldiers.'

"'Can I go there?' the boy asked.

"His aunt laughed. 'Oh, Tommy, you could never go there. That's for rich people.'"

It is a sad but true reality that preparing yourself for a competitive institution like a service academy takes money as well as time. If your family has the resources, you can get all kinds of experience that aren't necessarily available to someone in a family of more limited financial means. Clearly, not everybody starts from the same place, but Tommy's aunt was wrong: the academies are not only for rich people. (Tom Carhart successfully graduated from West Point and went on to serve in Vietnam.)

In appendix II, you'll find class profiles for the different academies. Take a look at the Naval Academy's profile under "Class Composition." Note that 21 percent fit into the category "Hardship or Adverse Life Experience." Only the Naval Academy breaks it out as a line item, but all the academies consider this as a factor.

If you've overcome hardship, you're demonstrating character, discipline, and leadership—exactly the sort of qualities that the academies welcome. If you work because your income is needed to support your family, for example, that counts as a leadership activity, and you get full points. And you've earned them.

So what do you do if you can't afford to do a lot of volunteer work because you have to bring in money to meet basic needs? What if you're responsible for siblings while a parent works and can't participate in the same range of extracurricular activities?

When you start your application process, contact your academy liaison officer early. Discuss your situation with the liaison officer and with your guidance counselor. Don't automatically expect that people understand your situation. Make sure you explain any special circumstances.

You'll be asked to arrange for letters of reference from specific high school teachers. Make sure the people who will be writing those letters know your situation, so they can include it in their letters.

Develop a network of adult mentors and supporters. These can include teachers and guidance professionals, religious and community figures, and much more. A network will help you through the process, and having a network also shows leadership skills on your part.

If your high school education hasn't prepared you for the rigors of an academy curriculum, but you have demonstrated potential in other ways, you may be offered admission to one of the preparatory schools rather than the main academy. While that means it will take you five years instead of four to graduate, that extra year will help fill in any gaps in your curriculum and develop the study and organizational skills to help you succeed.

DIVERSITY RECRUITING

The academies exist to train the officer corps for the different branches of the military. As a result, academies take their standards about whom they accept from the standards of the greater military. For a large part of American history, women, minorities, and LGBT people were excluded from the military, or allowed only in extremely restricted roles, and academy standards for admission reflected this.

Today, the academies actively seek highly qualified minority candidates, including African-Americans, Hispanics, Asians, and Native Americans.

While discrimination against African-Americans has been the most obvious, frequently backed up by laws, other minority groups have experienced issues as well. Diversity recruiting efforts include Hispanics, Asians, Native Americans, and others.

The first African-American cadets and midshipmen at the service academies encountered substantial discrimination and sometimes outright abuse. The first African-American West Point graduate Henry O. Flippin, Class of 1877, endured four years of silent treatment from the Corps of Cadets. At the Naval Academy, John Conyers was subject to physical abuse and even an attempt by his classmates to drown him. He left after a year.

In spite of that, a trickle of African-American cadets and midshipmen graduated from an academy in the decades following the American Civil War—making the academies relatively progressive for their time. Up until the early 1970s, however, black academy graduates were still a rarity. Although the US military had officially desegregated by presidential order in 1949, blacks were mostly relegated to enlisted ranks. Racial strife in the 1970s led the Department of Defense to the realization that it was vital for national security for the officer corps to resemble the military as a whole, making diversity a high operational priority.

Within a decade, minority enrollment hit new heights, and the current classes (at the time of writing) have the highest level of minority enrollment in their history.

In terms of your chances to get in, the rate at which people of different racial or ethnic backgrounds are admitted to the academies tracks pretty closely to their percentage in the applicant pool. Graduation rates for cadets and midshipmen are comparable across racial, ethnic, and gender lines; in fact, they're higher than in comparable civilian institutions.

> **SPECIAL NOTE!** Diversity recruiting does *not* mean that the academies lower their standards simply to attract minority candidates. Instead, it means that the academies actively seek out highly qualified minority candidates to urge them to apply, look at additional criteria (such as overcoming hardship) as evidence of leadership potential, and use the prep schools as a way to help otherwise highly qualified candidates whose academic preparation has been deficient.

Sadly, some opportunities for minority candidates go unfilled. Members of Congress in heavily minority areas rank toward the bottom in the number of nominations they make. Some of this can be attributed to struggling schools and a lack of awareness. In response, the academies have been working with certain members to improve outreach to find high potential nominees.

If you are a potential minority candidate, begin by reaching out to the diversity program office for the academy in which you're interested, as shown in table 6-2.

Table 6-2.   Diversity Program Websites

Academy	Contact
West Point	www.usma.edu/admissions/sitepages/diversity_outreach.aspx
Naval Academy	No specific diversity website. Contact your Blue and Gold Officer as part of the admissions process.
Coast Guard Academy	www.cga.edu/about.aspx?id=32
Merchant Marine Academy	www.usmma.edu/admissions/diversity
Air Force Academy	www.academyadmissions.com/admissions/outreach-programs/diversity-outreach/

WOMEN

The attitude of the military toward women soldiers has changed substantially over the years. The first women were admitted to the academies in 1976 and had to battle substantial male prejudice. That battle is not over, but there has been major progress on that front.

The biggest barrier to women at academies has been the policy that women were restricted from most combat roles. Now that this policy has been relaxed and in many cases eliminated, women have been entering the academies in greater numbers each year.

Academic standards and requirements for male and female candidates are the same. On the Candidate Fitness Assessment (CFA), the average scores for women are lower than the average scores for men, but all applicants must meet minimum standards of fitness. The one specific difference is that women who cannot perform a single pull-up may substitute the flexed-arm hang instead.

For information on what it's like to be a woman at a military academy, seek out current or former cadets. If you're looking at West Point, you might check out the organization West Point Women at www.westpointwomen.org.

LGBT

Gays, lesbians, bisexuals, and transgendered people have served in the military throughout history, although seldom openly. General Friedrich von Steuben, a key figure in developing the fledgling Colonial army into an effective fighting force during the American Revolutionary War, had fled Prussia under threat of being prosecuted for homosexuality.

With the establishment of "Don't Ask, Don't Tell" (DADT) in 1993, it was no longer forbidden for lesbians, gays, and bisexuals to serve, but they were not allowed to serve openly. In 2011, a court barred further enforcement of the policy. As a result, openly gay, lesbian, and bisexual cadets now attend all the service academies. Being in this category is unlikely to have any effect on your chance of admission because the admissions committee won't know unless you make a point of telling them. If your leadership experience comes from being president of the Gay Student Union at your high school, it may be appropriate to tell them; otherwise not. When homosexuality was disqualifying, there were questions in the medical evaluation about it. Those questions are no longer there.

If you are trans or genderqueer, on the other hand, you do have a problem. Current Department of Defense medical regulations list "transsexual, gender identity disorder, and change of sex (or attempt to change sex)" as disqualifying. Any surgery or medication will show up as part of the medical evaluation process, and you will be asked about trans orientation on the psychological portion of the questionnaire. At the time of writing, the secretary of defense has ordered a review of this policy, but it remains in effect until changed.

If possible, talk with people who share your orientation and who have attended an academy. The Service Academy Gay and Lesbian Alumni Association (http://sagala.net) is a good place to start. There are chapters for each of the academies, as well as on-campus clubs where you can find support after admission.

RELIGIOUS PREFERENCE

A few years ago, there was a scandal at the US Air Force Academy involving inappropriate religious proselytizing and discrimination against people with less common (or no) religious beliefs.[2] While issues of religious discrimination still show up from time to time, in general the academies have worked to meet the diverse religious (or nonreligious) needs of the student population. We've provided some information in appendix III about different programs and offerings. You'll find information about Jewish worship, Muslim worship, and groups for nonbelievers.

Religious preference won't factor into admissions decisions. For one thing, they won't know your preference unless you tell them. You won't be asked about religion on your application. However, if your leadership or community experience involves work with religious groups, you should certainly provide the necessary information. After acceptance, you may be asked about religious preference so that the appropriate chaplains or groups are able to reach out to you.

FOREIGN/DUAL CITIZENSHIP

Except for the small number of foreign cadets and midshipmen discussed previously, you must be a US citizen to receive an appointment. If you are in the process of becoming a citizen, and will be a citizen by the time you would be admitted, you can apply. Make sure your academy liaison officer is up to date on your status.

A certain number of people have dual citizenship, in which you are both a US citizen and a citizen of another country. For ordinary purposes, this is not a problem, but in order to enter an academy, you will have to renounce your non-US citizenship.

You'll need to disclose the dual citizenship during the applications process, and tell your academy liaison officer about it. Make clear that you are willing to renounce the other citizenship; if you aren't willing, they won't be able to admit you. Don't rush to renounce the citizenship before you're accepted. In the case of West Point, we received an information packet (sent to all admitted cadets) directing anyone with dual citizenship to work with a specific academy official charged with navigating the process. The reason is that renouncing citizenship can be complicated, and if it's done incorrectly can create huge and unnecessary problems. Let them guide you through the process and follow their instructions.

HOMESCHOOLED OR NONTRADITIONAL EDUCATION

The basic application system is designed for people who attended a regular public or private high school, but if you were homeschooled or have a nontraditional education, you are still eligible to apply and will be considered on the same basis as everybody else. However, it's up to you to make sure that the academy has enough information to evaluate you fully. Search each academy website for "homeschoolers" to get all the necessary information.

If you're homeschooled, the academies will place greater weight on your standardized test scores as a proxy for overall academic performance. It's useful for your home school to be recognized by your local school board or other official body, though not mandatory.

You need to prepare a transcript that shows you have done all the required coursework, including a description of the curriculum, text or other materials used, length of course, and how well you did. The academies recommend, but don't require, that you take some junior college or college level courses to demonstrate your ability to perform in a group classroom setting.

The academies require teacher evaluations. These can be done by junior college or college teachers, private tutors, or others familiar with your work.

Above all, *focus on extracurricular and community activities that demonstrate athletic ability and leadership*! The single biggest problem homeschoolers face is weakness in these areas, so make it a priority to find group sports to participate in or community activities where you can demonstrate your leadership potential and your ability to work well with others.

The Air Force Academy has an excellent and very detailed pamphlet for homeschooled students: www.academyadmissions.com/wp-content/uploads/2012/05/homeschool_pamphlet.pdf. It's a useful document no matter which academy you're considering.

TROUBLE

Teenagers, even ones who eventually grow up to be fine upstanding citizens, have been known to get into trouble from time to time. You will be asked about drug and alcohol abuse, any criminal record, or serious trouble at school. If you have to answer "Yes," are you out of the running? Not necessarily. That's according to Col. Deborah McDonald, director of admissions at West Point.

"One instance of bad judgment shouldn't ruin your entire life," she said. "The question we have is what you did with that experience. Has it caused you to change your life in a positive way? Tell us about that." She went on to explain that the ability to overcome failure and setbacks is an important ingredient in a cadet and in a military officer. "Sometimes, people who have never messed up or failed don't know how to handle it when it eventually happens."

Let's look at some specific categories.

Drug and Alcohol Use

If you smoked marijuana once or twice or had an underage drink or two, it won't automatically disqualify you from an academy appointment, but lying about it certainly will—even if they don't find out until after you've been admitted.

You will be asked about drug and alcohol use on the medical questionnaire. A "Yes" answer will need to be explained, but if your usage is both minor and in the past, you should be all right.

You will also be drug tested when you arrive at the academy. Every year, in spite of clear warnings, a couple of people fail the urine test and end their academy career before it starts.

Encounters with Law Enforcement

One requirement for admission is "good moral character," and that implies lack of a criminal record. You'll be asked about any criminal record during the application process, and after admission you'll be required to get a Secret security clearance, which will involve a detailed check with your local police department. If you've been arrested, even if you weren't convicted, that will show up. If you've had a speeding ticket or two, that's not necessarily a problem, but a DUI is likely to be fatal to your service academy hopes. Felonies are pretty much fatal.

If there are extenuating circumstances or special conditions, prepare a statement and speak with your academy liaison officer. Make sure you have any documentation, letters, or other materials available. Remember that what you did about your mistake can matter as much as the mistake itself, so be ready to explain how you've changed. It's not enough to *say* you've learned your lesson, you need to back it up. Deeds speak louder than words.

Problems in School

Problems in middle or elementary school are pretty safe to ignore, but once you're in high school, you'll have to come clean about suspensions or other major trouble. Again, if the trouble happened early in your high school career, and your subsequent behavior and record has demonstrated your change and growth, you may be able to overcome it.

FORMER CADETS

The Air Force Academy has written procedures for former cadets seeking readmission to the academy at www.academyadmissions.com/wp-content/uploads/2012/05/Information_for_Ex-cadets.pdf. For other academies, contact the admissions office or an admission liaison.

7

Candidate Fitness Assessment and Medical Clearance

While the volume of applications to academies has risen over the years, the number of qualified candidates has shrunk. The problem isn't academics or even leadership, but rather physical fitness. "The youth in America are becoming heavier and heavier, and, in some cases, obese," said West Point admissions director Col. Deborah McDonald.[1]

Service academy cadets and midshipmen are expected to be well above average in strength, endurance, and agility. Well over 90 percent of admitted candidates have a varsity letter in at least one sport (and at least half were team captain), and you should be among them.

In addition, there are two other ways that you demonstrate your physical fitness and health: the Candidate Fitness Assessment (CFA), and medical clearance through the Department of Defense Medical Review Board (DoDMERB).

While preparing for the CFA is fairly straightforward—practice, practice, and practice!—the medical clearance process often turns into one of the most stressful parts of your application. You can't start the DoDMERB process until the academy says so, but you can start making sure you've got all the necessary paperwork ready to go.

CANDIDATE FITNESS ASSESSMENT

The Candidate Fitness Assessment is a test of your muscular strength and endurance, cardio-respiratory endurance, power, balance, and agility. It consists of a series of events that must be performed in a certain order and in a fixed amount of time, which create a cumulative loading effect. That means you won't do as well on the final events as you did in training. That's built into the scoring system.

You'll find the instructions for the CFA on each academy website. If you're applying to more than one academy, you only need one CFA; they're identical across the board.

Usually, you're on your own when it comes to arranging for your CFA exam. If you're attending one of the academy summer programs between your junior and senior year of high school, you'll have an opportunity to complete your CFA while you're there.

The CFA is required by all the academies except for the Coast Guard, which has its own version, called the Physical Fitness Exam (PFE). You can find information on the PFE at www.cga.edu/admissions2.aspx?id=80. (If you've already done the CFA for another academy, you are permitted to submit the CFA instead, but the Coast Guard Academy highly recommends you take the PFE.)

How the CFA Works

There are six parts to the CFA. They must be completed in the specified order. There are time limits for individual exercises and a time limit for the test as a whole. The test is graded pass/fail. That means you must get the minimum acceptable score for each individual exercise and a minimum cumulative score for the entire assessment.

You need to do your very best, because the academies don't tell you what the passing scores are! Instead, you're given two pieces of information: the maximum score and the average score for each event (table 7-1).

SPECIAL NOTE! Although the CFA is graded pass/fail, the academies don't tell you what the passing scores are, so it's important to do your very best!

Table 7-1. Benchmarks for the Candidate Fitness Assessment

Exercise	Men		Women	
	Maximum	Average	Maximum	Average
Basketball Throw	102'	69'	66'	41'
Pull-Ups (men or women)	18	12	7	3
Flexed-Arm Hang (women only)			63 sec.	24 sec.
Shuttle Run	7.6 sec.	8.9 sec.	8.6 sec.	9.7 sec.
Modified Sit-Ups (crunches)	95	81	95	78
Push-Ups	75	61	50	41
One Mile Run	5:20	6:36	6:00	7:35

If you're average or above average in all of the categories, it's a pretty safe bet that you're above the pass line. If you're below average in one or two of the categories, you're probably okay as long as you're not too far below average and if you're above average in other categories. Points for being above average in a category add to your total score, and that can put you across the finish line as long as your worst scores are still above the (secret) minimum.

Taking the CFA

You have to make the necessary arrangements to take the CFA; the academies don't do it for you. Fortunately, it's often possible to arrange to take the test in your own school, and you have a lot of flexibility about when you decide to take it. (This is useful if you need more time to train for it.)

Here's what you need to do.

Preparation

First, find someone eligible to be a CFA Administrator. An eligible administration can be a physical education teacher, a military academy liaison officer, a military officer or noncommissioned officer, a professor of military science, or a J/ROTC instructor. (You should *not* use the coach for your particular sport.) Your CFA Administrator will need to recruit help, because it takes more than one person to administer some of the events.

If you're asking a physical education (P.E.) teacher at your school to be your test administrator, that person may or may not know anything about the CFA. You should download a copy of the CFA instructions and print it out for your prospective test administrator.

SPECIAL NOTE! Find the CFA instruction PDF here: www.usma.edu/admissions/shared%20documents/cfa_instructions.pdf. There is also a video on YouTube for CFA Administrators at www.youtube.com/watch?v=AlIZz9O7QiQ. Although these are both from West Point, the CFA is the same for all academies except Coast Guard.

Ask the eligible person if he or she is willing to administer the test, and if so, you'll enter that person's contact information online through your candidate portal. The administrator will get an email with instructions of how to submit your results.

Next, you need a site to administer the test. Ideally, the site will have an indoor gymnasium and an outdoor track next to each other. The timing allows eight minutes to go from the gym to the track for your one-mile run. If you can't make that happen, the one-mile run can be administered indoors as well.

Third, the test requires some equipment: a sit-up mat, a 100-foot tape measure, two stop watches, a regulation basketball, and a pull-up bar. For the one-mile run, whether it's on an outdoor track or just running around the gym, the surface needs to be flat and free of debris. If it's indoors, the distance has to be carefully measured.

Finally, the test administrator is responsible for preparing the site. (You can help, of course.) The instructions contain all the necessary information.

Testing Procedures

You can do practice tests as many times as you like, as long as the facility is available and your test administrator is willing. However, once you decide to take the real test, there's no turning back. Officially, you're only entitled to one try, but if your test administrator is willing, you might be able to retake it before your scores are submitted. Sometimes, an academy will ask you to retake the CFA if you're otherwise competitive but fall short on the physical test. That's up to them, however. Academies have different policies on retaking, and those policies have been known to change, so check.

Wear normal gym-type clothes for the test: shorts, T-shirt, socks, and running shoes. (They recommend you don't use tennis or basketball shoes.) You can't wear anything else, such as a weight belt, unless it's medically prescribed. If you will be running outdoors in cold weather, you can wear clothes appropriate to the weather.

The instructions suggest that you spend 20–30 minutes in active warm-up and stretching prior to beginning the test. Once you're ready, the test administrator reads the instructions aloud, and when that's done, the test begins. From this moment on, you're on the clock until it's over.

Table 7-2 shows the sequence and timeline for the CFA.

The Test

Basketball Throw

The infamous basketball throw has intimidated CFA candidates for many years. It's not exactly something you do in regular sports, but it's

Table 7-2. CFA Sequence and Timeline

Event	Test Start Time	Testing Time	Rest	Total Time
Basketball Throw	0 minutes	2 minutes	3 minutes	5 minutes
Cadence Pull-Ups/				
Flexed-Arm Hang	5 minutes	2 minutes	3 minutes	10 minutes
Shuttle Run	10 minutes	2 minutes	3 minutes	15 minutes
Modified Sit-Ups	15 minutes	2 minutes	3 minutes	20 minutes
Push-Ups	20 minutes	2 minutes	8 minutes (includes getting from gym to track)	30 minutes
One-Mile Run	30 minutes	Until completed		Until completed

still a valuable test of your total body coordination and balance, along with a demonstration of shoulder strength.

Basically, you kneel down with your knees parallel to a baseline. You take the basketball and throw it overhand as far as you can in a more or less straight line. The distance of the throw is measured by when the ball first hits the floor. You get three tries, and your best distance gets recorded.

Cadence Pull-Ups or Flexed-Arm Hang

Cadence Pull-Ups. Start on the pull-up bar with the backs of your hands facing you, arms fully extended in a "dead hang." For each pull-up, raise your body until your jaw is parallel to the ground and above the bar. You can't swing, kick, or bicycle your legs. Your test administrator will call the number of each repetition as soon as you've done this, and that's your signal to lower your arms back to "dead hang" position. If your pull-up doesn't meet the standards, the test administrator doesn't count it.

This test lasts two minutes, and when the two minutes are up, the test administrator will tell you to stop. Your score is the number of successful pull-ups you complete in that amount of time. If you achieve the maximum number of pull-ups before two minutes is up, the test administrator will tell you to stop.

Flexed-Arm Hang (females only). A woman who cannot complete even one cadence pull-up may substitute the flexed-arm hang instead. However, the way the scoring works, you get more points for a single cadence pull-up than you'll get from a flexed-arm hang, no matter how long you last.

Stand on a platform tall enough so that your chin is parallel to the floor and above the bar. Step off the platform and hang there as long as you can, up to the maximum. As with the pull-ups, you can't swing, kick, or bicycle your legs during the test.

Shuttle Run

In the shuttle run, you sprint thirty feet, touch the floor with your hand and foot simultaneously, turn around, and run back across the starting line. If you touch early, the trial doesn't count. You get two trials with a minute to rest in between; best time counts.

Modified Sit-Ups (Crunches)

Lie on your back, knees bent at about a ninety degree angle. Cross your arms with your fingers extended and touching the top of your shoulders. Your shoulder blades must touch the floor or sit-up mat. When the test administrator says "Go," flex from the hip and raise your elbows until they touch your thighs at midpoint or higher. Your fingertips have to stay in contact with your shoulders. An assistant holds your feet.

In two minutes, your job is to complete as many sit-ups as possible. The test administrator counts them out loud. If any sit-up doesn't meet the standards, the test administrator doesn't count it. If you need to rest, you can only rest in the "up" position. Resting while down ends the test. As with the pull-ups, if you meet the maximum before the two minutes are up, you're done. The administrator records your final score.

Push-Ups

Push-ups are, of course, a staple of military life. You'll do a lot of them if you go to an academy. Like the sit-ups, each repetition must be right or it doesn't count.

Start in a prone position, belly down, supported by one knee. On "Get set," place your hands just outside your shoulders with fingers forward. You can put your feet together, or you can extend them up to twelve inches apart, as you please. Your body should form a straight line from shoulders to ankles.

On "Go," bend your elbows to lower your entire body (still in a straight line) until your upper arms are at a minimum of a ninety-degree angle. Then push up until your arms are fully extended. If you need to rest, you must rest in the "up" position. You can flex your back while resting as long as you don't lift a hand or foot off the floor or let any other body part touch. After resting, return to the starting position before continuing your push-ups.

The test administrator counts the number of correct push-ups within two minutes. As before, if you hit the maximum, the test ends there.

One-Mile Run

You get three minutes to rest in between the previous exercises. You get eight minutes between finishing your push-ups and starting your one-mile run. This is supposed to give you enough time to get to the outdoor track. Get in position behind the starting line, and on the command "Go," start running until you've run a full mile. The final time goes on your score sheet.

If you need to walk a little bit, that's not disqualifying, but it will affect your final time. Walking, therefore, is "strongly discouraged." You can't get any physical help during the run; you can't leave the running course for any reason; and you can't have another person pace you.

Aftermath

At the end of the test, the administrator uploads your scores, following the instructions from the earlier email. That particular light on your portal will turn green, confirming that the CFA is done. A green light doesn't mean you necessarily passed, but only that the scores are in the system. It's your job, not the test administrator, to make sure the scores go through. If the portal doesn't show the scores are in after a couple of days, follow up.

> **SPECIAL NOTE!** If you're otherwise competitive, but your scores on one or more of the CFA tests are below the line, the academies may ask you to retake the test. That's up to the academy, though. It's best to assume you get one chance. Make sure it counts.

How to Prepare

No matter how physically fit you are, you need to prepare yourself for the Candidate Fitness Assessment. You need to practice each individual element of the test as well as practice completing the entire CFA in the proper order. Because the process is designed to test your endurance, you're probably not going to achieve the scores in later events that you can hit in practice doing them individually. Remember, the test-scoring process takes this into account.

You'll find a selection of articles and videos in appendix III that will help you prepare yourself. Talk with your coach about any fitness regimen he or she might recommend. If you are participating in a varsity sport, whether or not you're trying to become a recruited athlete, try to take the CFA in the summer or at least outside the season for your sport. If you're hurt or injured, wait until you're at your best before taking it.

> **SPECIAL NOTE!** Practice, practice, practice! Even if you're an outstanding athlete, the CFA can still be harder than you expect.

MEDICAL CLEARANCE (DoDMERB)

The medical clearance process, generally known as DoDMERB for the agency that administers it (Department of Defense Medical Review Board), can end up as one of the most nerve-wracking and difficult parts of the applications process. You must go through the DoDMERB process for all service academies as well as for four-year ROTC programs. With luck, you'll sail through the process without issues, get your rating of "Qualified," and move ahead. If not, don't give up yet. There's still hope.

Often problems in medical clearance come as a surprise to candidates. Worse, by the time you start the medical clearance process, it's already fairly late in the applications cycle, giving you little time to resolve any issues.

Here's what happened to us. My son was hurt playing high school football and went to the emergency room (ER) with severe back pain. The ER physician ordered an X-ray, and the radiologist reported that he had a problem with his spine. This was very serious indeed, and for a little bit we feared that his attempt to get into an academy was over before it got started.

The next day, we took him to a pediatric orthopedist, fearing the worst, but the orthopedist wasn't worried. He looked at the X-rays and told us that the ER diagnosis was wrong. It was just a back sprain, painful but temporary. For good measure, he ordered an MRI, and that came back clean as well to everybody's relief.

One of the questions on the DoDMERB forms asked whether he'd ever experienced back pain, and he answered yes. He explained the situation to the physician who examined him.

A week or so later, his candidate portal was updated with the DoDMERB results. His classification was "Remedial," meaning that DoDMERB required additional information before deciding whether he was medically qualified. A letter arrived a day or so later asking him to submit "all medical records concerning back pain."

One of those records, of course, was the emergency room report stating that he had a spinal injury. Although we knew the diagnosis was incorrect, he was still obligated to submit the report. It was late January, and the applications process closed at the end of February. If he had to go through a medical disqualification and a rebuttal process, it could potentially take months.

The next two weeks were a flurry of doctor visits and photocopying, and he ended up with a huge packet of information to send to DoDMERB, along with a detailed letter explaining what had happened, along with references to the specific information that supported his claim.

Fortunately, that did the trick. Within a week, his candidate portal updated with the new information: he was medically qualified.

SPECIAL NOTE! Review the DoDMERB forms and questions as early as you can, even before the academy orders your evaluation. If you anticipate problems, you have time to organize any information you will need. This can be very helpful in those stressful days as your application enters its final stage.

DoDMERB Outcomes

All the service academies as well as ROTC use DoDMERB to perform medical evaluations of all candidates for admission. Except for vision standards, which vary slightly, the other medical standards are identical for all services and academies.

Qualified. The happiest DoDMERB result is *medically qualified.* As long as nothing physically bad happens to you between now and the time you report, you're good to go. (If you do experience a medical problem, you have to notify DoDMERB and go through the process again.)

Remedial. If DoDMERB needs more information to make its decision, your status will be *remedial.* An *administrative remedial* means that you have to send them all medical records related to whatever issue concerns them. A *medical remedial* means that DoDMERB wants additional medical tests before they make their decision. You're responsible for gathering any information related to an administrative remedial, and that's done at your own expense. If DoDMERB requires a medical remedial, the military will pay for those additional tests if you go to the provider they choose; if you choose your own provider, you pay.

Disqualified. You will be rated *disqualified* if you don't meet all the medical requirements, but don't despair quite yet. DoDMERB is required to administer the medical standards strictly and without exception. However, the academies may, if they choose, waive certain disqualifications and admit you anyway. That's up to the academies, not up to DoDMERB.

Waiver. If DoDMERB rates you as disqualified, you are automatically considered for a *waiver*. A waiver means that you have the condition, but the academies have decided that you are admissible in spite of it. You don't have to apply for a waiver, but they don't have to grant it either. First, your file is sent back to the admissions department. They decide whether you would be likely to be admitted if not for the medical issue. If the admissions department has already decided you aren't competitive, the process ends there.

If you are competitive, your medical records get sent to the staff physicians at the academy. Unlike DoDMERB, which is required to follow the rules without exception, the academy doctors use their best judgment to decide whether the medical issue is such that you wouldn't be able to complete the academy program, or serve as a military officer following graduation. Many conditions that technically disqualify you under DoDMERB may not be serious enough to stop your academy hopes. If the academy doctors decide it's not too serious, they issue a waiver, and the admissions process continues.

SPECIAL NOTE! The DoDMERB process is the same for all academies. If you are applying to multiple academies, you only need one DoDMERB exam. However, waivers are decided by the academies, not DoDMERB, and each academy makes its own individual decision. It is very possible to receive a waiver from one academy and be denied a waiver for the very same condition from another academy, because the needs of each service vary.

Rebuttal. In general, arguing with DoDMERB is not likely to get you very far. They have no flexibility where the rules are concerned. However, it's possible that you, like my son, have received a medical diagnosis that's incorrect, or have a condition that no longer exists. In that case, you can submit information to DoDMERB to demonstrate that the diagnosis is wrong. If DoDMERB agrees, they will change your rating to qualified, and you no longer have to worry about getting a waiver. (What we did in my son's case might be considered a "pre-buttal," because we sent in rebuttal-type information before a "disqualified" rating was issued in the first place.)

Rebuttals are used for cases in which a diagnosis in your file is wrong or out of date—that you do not have the condition they say you have. Don't use the rebuttal process to argue that the medical standards or processes are wrong. DoDMERB does not have the authority to change Department of Defense medical policy, and it's a waste of everybody's time to fight about it.

Preparing for DoDMERB

You can visit the DoDMERB website at https://DoDMERB.tricare. osd.mil/ and download some preliminary information even if your academy has not yet ordered your examination. Start with the link labeled "Questions on the Process?" and you'll find an extremely useful memorandum that describes the process and includes instructions on how to get help if you need it. It's also got advice about what kind of information may help you and what will not. (For example, letters from your coach about what a great athlete you are, or any other nonmedical opinions, won't be given very much credence.)

You can download a number of the preliminary forms and look them over to see if there are issues that might give rise to concerns. There are separate questionnaires for allergies, head injuries, headaches, vision problems, and mental health/behavioral concerns. There's a link to a list of medical codes, one a list of disqualification codes and the other a list of remedial codes (requests for more information and additional tests that may be ordered). Look them over for any major concerns. If you need more information, you can consult the official Department of Defense standard, known as DoDI 6130.03.[2] (You may see references to DoDI 6130.4 in some places; the 6130.03 regulation replaces it.)

If you have "yes" answers to any of these questions, or if you have any of the conditions with disqualifying codes, it's never too early to gather together all the necessary medical records. The more quickly and more thoroughly you're able to respond to DoDMERB, the better. If you do receive a disqualification, having the information available makes it easier for the academy doctors to evaluate whether you should receive a waiver.

If you have any conditions that can be corrected (certain dental problems, for example), get them taken care of before you get the directive to start the process. Frankly, this is a good idea whether or not you go to an academy.

Height and Weight

Your height and weight must fall within an appropriate range. You'll be measured during your DoDMERB physical and again on arrival day at the academy, so keep an eye on your weight.

All the services except for the Coast Guard require that your height be at least 58 inches (4 feet 10 inches) and no more than 80 inches (6 feet 8 inches). The Coast Guard has a minimum height requirement of 60 inches (5 feet) for males, 58 inches for women, with the same maximums.

Weight requirements, however, vary by service, so you'll need to check with each academy or search online for service height and weight standards, especially if you fall close to the borderline. The Coast Guard adjusts their numbers based on body frame type, further complicating the picture. Because Merchant Marine Academy graduates receive a Naval Reserve commission, they must meet the Navy standard.

Table 7-3 shows the variation in weight standards for men and women who are 68" (5'8") tall and between 17 and 20 years of age. The first number is the minimum and the second number is the maximum.

If you don't meet the weight standard for your height, you can still qualify if your body fat percentage is below the number for your service and gender. Body fat percentages are independent of height.

Table 7-3. Weight Standards by Service for 68-Inch Height

Service	Army		Navy		Marine Corps		Air Force	
Gender	Men	Women	Men	Women	Men	Women	Men	Women
Min./Max. Weight	125/ 170	125/ 164	125/ 181	125/ 170	125/ 181	125/ 164	125/ 180	125/ 180
Max. Body Fat	20%	30%	25%	35%	18%	26%	20%	28%

Medical Red Flags

There are a number of common issues that crop up in the DoDMERB process. If any of these apply to you, be prepared. In some cases, a diagnosis may have been made for casual reasons rather than based on a thorough evaluation. Some conditions that are otherwise disqualifying may have special exceptions or qualifications in the regulations that apply to you. In other cases, the condition isn't disqualifying, but

DoDMERB will probably ask for additional information in order to reach its decision. Have it ready if at all possible.

This is not a comprehensive list by any means. If you know you have an issue not listed, consult DoDI 6130.03.

If you do have one of these conditions, and you don't fall into one of the exceptions, you should expect to be disqualified. Remember, though, that a DoDMERB disqualification isn't the end of the matter. The academies, not DoDMERB, make the final decision through the waiver process.

SPECIAL NOTE! Whether you get a waiver for a disqualifying condition depends on individual circumstances and the needs of the services at any particular time. When it comes to waivers, the official word is "never say always, and never say never."

Asthma, Seasonal Allergies, Inhaler Use

Asthma is automatically disqualifying, but seasonal allergies aren't necessarily a problem if they aren't too severe. If you have been diagnosed with asthma past your thirteenth birthday, or have had a prescription for an inhaler for asthma after your thirteenth birthday (even if you never used it), you will be disqualified. (Anything before your thirteenth birthday doesn't count.) There is an exception in the regulations for people who haven't used any medications, haven't had any severe attacks, and have a recent normal spirometry. Check DoDI 6130.03 for details.

Sometimes, doctors have been known to write down a diagnosis of asthma when the condition really falls in the category of seasonal allergies. If you have been asymptomatic for a long time but keep an inhaler around "just in case" (even if you never used it), it's a good idea to find out whether you really *do* have asthma.

Remember, if your medical records say you have asthma, even if later diagnosis says you don't, you'll still have to share that information with DoDMERB. You'll want to have any rebuttal information handy so you can submit it.

Learning Disabilities and Other Mental Health Issues

Attention Deficit Hyperactivity Disorder (ADHD) is a disqualifying condition. While ADHD is real, there have been cases where the diagnosis was not based on a full medical assessment. If you're not sure whether you really do have ADHD, you need to get the necessary evaluations and associated documentation. If you don't have ADHD, but have the condition listed in your medical records, you'll need to disclose the earlier diagnosis, so you'll want to have any rebuttal documentation in hand.

Even if you do have ADHD, you won't be disqualified as long as you meet certain conditions listed in DoDI 6130.03. If you had problems in elementary school but they went away, and you haven't had any issues past age fourteen, you should be fine.

Other learning disorders, such as dyslexia, are disqualifying unless you have demonstrated acceptable academic and employment performance without accommodations past the age of fourteen.

Mental health issues, including developmental disorders, psychosis or schizophrenia, major depression, impulse control disorders, eating disorders, suicide attempts, and the like may be disqualifying depending on the severity. Merely seeing a psychologist isn't a problem; the academies themselves keep mental health professionals on staff to work with cadets and midshipmen as they deal with the ups and downs of military life. However, you may be asked to provide records. (You will also be asked about any counseling on your security clearance application. You must disclose it, but seeing a counselor by itself will not disqualify you.)

While being gay is no longer an issue, transsexuality is currently on the list of disqualifying psychosexual conditions.

Vision

DoDMERB won't disqualify you for needing glasses as long as your vision can be corrected to 20/20, but if your vision isn't perfect, you may not qualify for pilot training. Color blindness is disqualifying. Lasik or other kinds of eye surgery are frequently disqualifying; if you're thinking about it, don't. (Interestingly, you can have Lasik done while in the military.)

There are some individual differences in vision requirements among the services, so be sure to check the details on the appropriate academy websites. Because of the need for pilots, the Naval and Air Force Academies are a bit stricter than the Army.

Surgery, Concussions, and Head Injuries.

Surgery, concussions, or head injuries may or may not be disqualifying, depending on the circumstances. However, you should expect DoDMERB to ask for medical records and other documentation, so be prepared. Be sure to tell your medical providers that you are applying to a service academy.

If your surgery was recent (within the past six months), you may end up with a disqualification even if you are expected to heal completely. Decisions about whether you will have healed enough by the time you report are usually made by the academies through the waiver process. In some cases, you may end up disqualified for the year, but will be eligible to try again next year.

Medications

You'll be asked about any medications you take. The medications themselves aren't a problem; DoDMERB's concern is with the underlying medical condition. Some medications are known to have potential side effects that could produce a disqualifying condition. Check with your doctor.

Non-Medical Issues

Drug and Alcohol Use

While DoDMERB does not test for drug use, they will ask you about drug and alcohol use. (You *will* be tested for drug use when you report to the academy. A few candidates every year wash out on the very first day for exactly that reason.) Minor use of marijuana or a couple of drinks isn't a big deal; lying about it is. While you might get away with it initially, remember that military officers frequently need high-level security clearances, sometimes involving a polygraph test. Past dishonesty make come back to haunt you later.

Tattoos, Brands, Piercings, and Body Modifications

You'll be examined for any tattoos, unusual piercings, or other body modifications, and examined again when you report to the academy. In general, tattoos can't be visible when in uniform; can't be offensive, racist, gang-related, or "prejudicial to good order and discipline"; and can't cover large areas of the body. Women may have a single piercing in each ear; men may not have piercings. If you have any tattoos or piercings that fall outside the policy, you'll need to take care of them.

There are some slight variations in tattoo policy among the services; consult table 7-4 to find the specific policy for the appropriate service.

Table 7-4. Tattoo Policies

Academy	Tattoo Policy
West Point	www.usma.edu/admissions/sitepages/faq_admission.aspx
Naval Academy	www.usna.edu/AdminSupport/_files/documents/ instructions/6000-6999/6240.10B.pdf
Coast Guard Academy	www.uscga-district-7.org/hrdept/Member%20Processing/ CI_1000_1BTattos%20Body%20Piercing.pdf
Merchant Marine Academy	No published policy; use Naval Academy standards.
Air Force Academy	www.usafa.af.mil/questions/topic.asp?id=972

The Medical Evaluation Process

Putting a candidate through the medical evaluation process costs money, so the academies won't order the examination until they've decided that you're a competitive candidate. That's one more reason to get your application completed as soon as possible.

You'll be notified through your candidate portal, and given instructions about setting up your appointments. You will see a general physician and an optometrist. You'll also get some information from your regular dentist. (After acceptance, you'll need to send a complete set of dental X-rays to the academy. That's one of the few things you won't simply upload to your candidate portal; you'll need to mail it in.)

The Exam

Set up the appointments as soon as you can. You'll need to complete a number of forms beforehand, all of which are on the DoDMERB website, so give yourself the necessary time. (If you've followed the advice previously given, you've already gotten a head start on those forms.)

Throughout the process, answer all questions completely and honestly, even if you think they will raise red flags. Many medical issues can be resolved; dishonesty is likely to be fatal to your academy prospects or come back to haunt you later in your military career.

The physician and the optometrist will each go through a standardized evaluation procedure and fill out a form. Normally, you'll see doctors who are contracted by DoDMERB to perform these examinations, but you may also take exams at a military treatment facility (most common if you are in the service already).

DoDMERB Web Portal

Once you have taken your exam, you'll be given log-on instruction to the DoDMERB website so you can check your status. Check it regularly. Note that the DoDMERB website is a separate system from your candidate portal. Your candidate portal will show the final DoD-MERB results, but all the in-process information will only be on the DoDMERB website.

While the medical professionals you see are supposed to submit the information directly to DoDMERB, it's still your responsibility to be sure everything gets there.

Your contract physicians should submit their information automatically, but if you go through a military treatment facility, you're responsible for ensuring the information gets to DoDMERB. Either way, you're responsible for making sure the information gets there.

If too much time passes between the exam and getting information on the website (a week or so should be adequate), follow up with DoDMERB directly. You can find the necessary contact information in the "Questions on the Process?" memo mentioned earlier. In spite of the high volume of candidates being processed each year, DoDMERB is surprisingly responsive if you've got an issue.

Evaluation and Decision

Once DoDMERB has reviewed your examination results, they'll post their decisions: qualified, disqualified, or remedial. If you're qualified, you're done—unless something happens between then and when you report to the academy. If you're disqualified, it's now in the hands of the academy. However, if you have reason to believe that there is an error of some sort, you can offer a rebuttal in hopes DoDMERB will reconsider. You will be given a medical code that gives the reason for your disqualification.

If you get a remedial notice, check the list of codes. You will be asked either to submit additional information (administrative remedial) or asked to take additional tests (medical remedial). You're responsible for the administrative remedial (including costs associated with getting copies of medical records).

If DoDMERB requires additional tests, you have two choices. You can go to the DoDMERB-contracted medical provider and DoDMERB will pay for the tests, or you can have your own medical provider conduct the test, in which case you pay for it. Sometimes you aren't given the option and DoDMERB will require that you undergo the tests at a military treatment facility.

The decisions and actions will be provided on the DoDMERB website, sent to you in a letter, and sent to the academies to which you are applying.

Problems after the Examination

A "qualified" rating from DoDMERB means you were healthy at the time of the examination, but it's not necessarily the end of the process. If you get a concussion, break a bone, come down with pneumonia, or experience any other significant change in your health between that initial determination and the day you report to the academy, you're required to inform DoDMERB, and they will reassess your status. Each year, unfortunately, a few people get accepted, have an accident of some sort, and become medically disqualified. If this happens, the academy may or may not hold your slot until the following year. If not, you'll have to reapply and go through the process again.

If your parents threaten to wrap you in bubble wrap from the day you get accepted until they deliver you to the academy, now you know why.

Waivers and Rebuttals

A disqualification, as upsetting as it is, is not by any means the end of the process. Many candidates receive a disqualification notice from DoDMERB and still manage to get accepted by an academy. It's ultimately the academies, not DoDMERB, who decide whether to offer you admission.

If you get a "disqualified" rating from DoDMERB, you'll receive a letter giving the reason (along with the appropriate disqualification code). You'll be told whether the disqualification is "rebuttable" or "non-rebuttable," and given an outline of the procedure you need to follow.

If the condition is *rebuttable*, you may submit information to DoDMERB that proves (a) you never had the condition in the first place, (b) you did have the condition but you no longer have it, or (c) that you won't have the condition any longer by the time you report to the academy.

If it is *non-rebuttable*, DoDMERB will automatically send your file to the appropriate person in the admissions office for your academy so you can be considered for a waiver. You don't have to request that you be considered for a waiver, but by the same token, you can't force them to consider you for one.

Waivers are only granted by academies, never by DoDMERB itself. A waiver means that you have the disqualifying condition, but the academy has decided that it isn't bad enough to hamper your ability to complete your degree and discharge your service obligation after graduation.

There are no guarantees or certainties in the waiver process!
If you hear that someone with the same condition got a waiver, it
doesn't mean you will. Similarly, if you hear that someone with the
same condition was denied a waiver, it doesn't mean you will also be
denied. Waiting out the waiver process is, for some people, the single
most nerve-wracking part of the entire admissions process, and unfortunately there's not much to be done about it.

Timing

If you have a disqualification, it must be removed or waived before you
can be accepted, and in any case before you report to the academy. The
clock is ticking. That's why it's so important to get the DoDMERB
process underway as early as possible. However, the academies won't
order the DoDMERB evaluation until enough of your application is
complete so they can determine whether you are competitive enough
for admission. That's one more reason to stay on top of the applications process and get the entire thing done as early as you can.

That's not always possible, of course. That's why you should
follow the earlier advice in this chapter and look over your medical
history to see if you have any red flags, and if you do, start getting all
the information together. The more quickly and thoroughly you can
respond to any problems, the better.

Rebuttals

As discussed earlier, some conditions, such as asthma, are disqualifying unless you meet a list of criteria that demonstrate it's no longer
a problem. That's why a diagnosis of asthma is generally rebuttable.
Temporary conditions, such as healing from a broken bone, are also
usually rebuttable. You might well be disqualified today, but by the
time you report to the academy, you expect to be completely healed.

Other conditions are non-rebuttable, but that doesn't mean they
cannot be waived. For example, a history of depression may result in
a non-rebuttable disqualification not because DoDMERB thinks it's
an insurmountable issue but because the decision of how serious it is
should be left to the academy. (This is only an example; don't assume
that any history of depression will automatically be disqualifying or
determined to be non-rebuttable.)

DoDMERB decides what they consider rebuttable or non-rebuttable, and it's their choice, not yours and not the academy's. You should
remember, however, that just because DoDMERB says your disqualifi-

cation isn't rebuttable doesn't mean it can't be waived. Those are two completely different things.

Your letter of disqualification will explain the steps in the rebuttal process. Follow them exactly; the process will go much more smoothly and more quickly if you do. Don't hesitate to call DoDMERB for clarification or help if you need it.

Only medical evidence, not letters from your coach saying you're fit to play, will be considered. DoDMERB wants proof that (a) the original diagnosis was wrong, (b) the condition no longer exists, or (c) you won't have the condition by the time you are expected to report.

Waivers

If your condition is non-rebuttable, or if your rebuttal isn't accepted by DoDMERB, your file is automatically sent to the admissions officer for your particular region. If you're applying to more than one academy, DoDMERB informs each admissions office. That's automatic; you don't have to do anything to make that happen. (Of course, things occasionally do slip through the cracks, so continue to keep an eye on your DoDMERB portal as well as your candidate portal. If more than a couple of weeks go by without an update, call DoDMERB or your admissions liaison officer to follow up.)

The first step in the waiver process is to determine whether you're likely to be admitted if the medical problem is waived. If you're no longer considered a competitive candidate, your waiver request will be denied, and your admissions process stops right there. It's also possible that your waiver request will be deferred until later if your admissions file isn't complete and there isn't enough information to decide how competitive you are.

The seriousness of your disqualifying condition doesn't play a role in this; your admissions officers aren't doctors. If you're applying to multiple academies, each admissions office makes a separate decision. It is very possible to be denied waiver consideration by one academy and given consideration by another.

If you are determined to be a competitive candidate, your DoDMERB file gets sent to the academy's medical department for review. You now have the opportunity to submit additional information to support your request for a waiver.

Stay on top of this process! Follow up with your admissions liaison officer or your regional commander. Show continued interest, and respond rapidly to all requests for information. Being well-organized and responsive counts in your favor.

Send all information to DoDMERB, not to the academy! Even though the academy's medical professionals will decide whether you get a waiver, DoDMERB still coordinates the process. If additional tests are required, it will be DoDMERB, not the academy, who orders them. You can send copies of the information to the academy (check with your admissions liaison officer or regional commander) to speed the process, but all the official information goes through DoDMERB.

> **SPECIAL NOTE!** DoDMERB processes tens of thousands of candidates each year, which means an immense amount of paperwork. If you don't follow their instructions to the letter, you may end up with substantial and unnecessary delays. In particular, they require you put your name and Social Security number on every page you send them. If you will be sending them a lot of paper, print out stickers with that information to make your life easier. Adding a cover letter with a numbered list of all enclosures is a good idea as well, even if not required.

FOR MORE INFORMATION

A quick online search for "DoDMERB issues" will bring up a host of discussion boards, blogs, and other information of varying degrees of accuracy and reliability. Some of the information is quite useful, but don't believe anybody who says that condition X will definitely be waived or that it definitely will not be waived.

Don't forget that your medical clearance is subject to change if you have an accident or illness after you've been approved, and even after you've been accepted. You are required to inform DoDMERB of any significant changes to your health, and they can review and change your qualification status at any time until the moment you officially report for duty. If you break a leg after that, it's the academy's issue, not DoDMERB's.

8

Acceptances and Rejections

I FINISHED MY APPLICATION. NOW WHAT?

Once you've completed your application, applied for your nomination, and gone through the DoDMERB evaluation, it's now time for the academy admissions department to determine whether you get offered an appointment.

Of course, it's usually not quite that simple. For one thing, bits and pieces of your application take longer to complete than others, so you may still be rushing to get a few things done. Have you arranged for your school to submit seventh semester transcripts? Have you completed the steps for any DoDMERB remedials? Did all of your teacher references submit their evaluations, or do you need to follow up with them? Don't forget that you're responsible for making sure everything is complete—even the pieces that other people are supposed to do.

Your online application will show a red or green icon beside each item. As long as there are any red items, you cannot be admitted—yet, anyway. Because of such issues as resolving a DoDMERB disqualification or unavailability of seventh semester grades, you can have some red lights hanging on for no fault of your own. Even if it's not your fault, be proactive and get these things resolved. If your academy has decided they want you, they can sometimes help resolve final red light issues. Follow up with school guidance officials, keep in touch with your academy liaison officer, and check your candidate portal at least once a week.

> **SPECIAL NOTE!** Each academy has a "drop dead" date by which your applications must be completely finished. If you aren't done by that deadline, the academy normally drops you from further consideration. In some cases, such as pending DoDMERB waivers, they may choose to keep your file open past the deadline, but you should *not* count on that happening.

CANDIDATE VISITS

If at all possible, it's a great idea to get a firsthand view of academy life. While you can simply visit most colleges and universities whenever you like, you'll want to check your academy for any restrictions or limitations on your visit. If you're a recruited athlete or diversity candidate, you may be offered the opportunity to visit through these programs.

Check to see if you're eligible for an overnight visit, in which you sleep in the dorms, attend classes, and experience daily life at the academy. My son had already been accepted when he went up for his overnight visit and found it very helpful, even though he'd already made his decision.

> **SPECIAL NOTE!** If you visit after acceptance, use the time to take care of business, such as buying required shoes and boots and setting up a bank account.

LETTERS OF ASSURANCE

If you are a high potential candidate, the academy may send you a *Letter of Assurance* (LOA) even before your file is finished. A letter of assurance is an offer of a conditional appointment to the academy—*if* you successfully complete the rest of the admissions process.

An LOA is not binding on the academy, and your status continues to be evaluated, just like every other candidate. You still must get your nomination, pass the CFA, and get past DoDMERB, all while maintaining the same level of performance you've demonstrated so far.

One step below an LOA is a *Letter of Encouragement* (LOE). Unlike an LOA, an LOE is not a conditional offer of appointment, but simply a letter that informs you that you're a competitive candidate and urges you to keep going.

Who gets an LOA or LOE? If the preliminary assessment of your application suggests you'll be a shoo-in for admission, you may get one of these letters as a way of encouraging you to finish the process and to choose the academy as the place you most want to go.

Usually, you need to have most of your application complete very early. If your application isn't complete until shortly before the deadline, there's no point in giving you an LOA or LOE; you'll receive the final word soon enough. So, if you get one, that's great news, but if you don't get one, it's not necessarily a problem. Most admitted candidates never get one—my son didn't. The earliest you are likely to receive an LOA or LEO is September of your senior year.

If you are a recruited athlete, you may get a *National Letter of Intent* (NLI) instead of an LOA. National letters of intent are issued by NCAA Division I and Division II schools and follow NCAA policies and procedures. Once you sign an NLI, you've made a commitment to attend that institution, and other coaches are no longer allowed to recruit you. The institution, in turn, agrees to accept you, as long as you continue to meet their admissions standards. If you receive an NLI, you'll be given instructions on when and how to sign it. Wikipedia gives some general information about NLIs here: http://en.wikipedia .org/wiki/National_Letter_of_Intent.

Besides giving you assurance that you're likely to get in, LOAs, LOEs, and NLIs may make you eligible for overnight visits or other opportunities to learn more about academy life. The letter you receive will spell out any benefits that come with it.

TYPES OF ADMISSION

Colleges and universities have different procedures for processing and deciding on applicants.

Early Decision/Early Action. In an *early decision* program, you apply to your top choice school by a deadline significantly earlier than the regular deadline, and in turn the school gives you their decision quickly. Early decision is a binding commitment. By applying this way, you agree that if they take you, you will go. *Early action*, by contrast, also gives you an early deadline and promises you an early answer, but it's nonbinding.

None of the academies offer an early decision option. The Coast Guard Academy does offer early action,[1] with an application deadline of October 15, as opposed to the regular application deadline of January 15.

Rolling Admission. *Rolling admission* means that the school evaluates applications and makes decisions on candidates as soon as they receive the application. If a school offers rolling admissions, you should make every effort to get your application in early, because the supply of remaining slots is steadily decreasing.

At the time of writing, the Naval Academy[2] and the Merchant Marine Academy[3] offer rolling admission. West Point[4] and the Air Force Academy[5] used to, but don't any more. The Coast Guard Academy, as noted above, offers early action instead. These policies have changed in the past, so check the academy websites and the update PDF for this book for the most recent information.

WHEN WILL I HEAR?

Starting in November, there's a small trickle of acceptances. To be one of those early recipients, you'll have to have all your applications (including nominations and DoDMERB) done and be ranked among the top of the applicant list. Some recruited athletes also qualify.

Because most Congressional offices don't decide on their nominations until late November or even December, it's far more likely you won't hear until after the new year begins. Pay attention to the cutoff date for applications for the upcoming class. Once the cutoff date has passed, files that are incomplete get dropped from further consideration. (Occasional exceptions get made for incomplete DoDMERB waivers and other issues, but those decisions are up to the academies.) Right after that, the majority of offers get made.

Not everybody accepts an offer once it arrives. Some candidates applied to other academies and some to other colleges and universities. Some people change their minds and decline their offers. As the "no" answers trickle in, the next names on the list get offers. Occasionally, people get hurt or change their minds very late in the process, so a few candidates may get an offer as late as June.

HOW WILL I HEAR?

When the admissions department decides on a candidate, they first notify the nominating member of Congress. Some members of Congress like to call their accepted nominees personally to tell them of their offer. If your cell phone registers a strange phone number with a 202 area code, answer it.

Members of Congress have a couple of days to make the call. It's up to the individual member whether to call. Many don't; ours didn't. During the interim, the admissions department puts together the Big Fat Envelope (BFE) containing all the material that goes along with an acceptance and sends it out.

As soon as the Congressional waiting period ends, the academy will update your candidate portal with the news that you've been accepted. You will either accept or decline the appointment using the portal.

In my son's case, he was home with a cold that day. As I was walking to the mailbox, I got a call on my cell phone: it was my son. "I got in!" he shouted. By the time I got back inside the house, he had already accepted his appointment. The BFE arrived the following day.

While you might expect a packet stuffed with forms, the BFE we received had a very nice certificate in a presentation folder, a letter from the academy superintendent, and that was it. For the other forms and procedures, it was back to the candidate portal.

By the way, if you get offered a prep school appointment rather than an appointment to the academy, you'll find out the same way.

WHAT IF I DON'T GET IN?

If you don't get an offer, you'll find out two ways: through your candidate portal and through an envelope that's much smaller than the BFE.

Now it's time for your backup plan. The general advice for college applicants is that you should apply to at least three institutions: a stretch school (a long shot, but possible), a match school (your qualifications are well within the norms), and a safety school (your qualifications are safely above average). The academies (and most congressional nomination forms) ask you to list other schools to which you are applying, at least in part to make sure you don't put all your eggs in one basket.

If your heart is set on military service, you should apply for an ROTC scholarship and apply to backup schools known for quality ROTC programs. ROTC turns out far more officers than do the academies, and many go on to distinguished careers.

You can consider enlisting in a branch of the military and try to get into an academy that way. That might be the best bet if your high school record isn't everything it should be, and you believe you can prove yourself on the job. A related strategy is to join a National Guard or Reserve unit; they have academy nominations available too.

You can also plan to reapply to the academy next year. There are quite a few candidates who don't make it in the first time, but succeed on a second—or even a third—try. Talk with your liaison officer to see if you can get an honest assessment of where you stand. In some cases, you're better off accepting that it's unlikely to happen and that you should pursue other options.

On the other hand, you may have been considered fully qualified, but just didn't make the cut. If you're determined to attend an academy, you can try again the following year. While you have to compete for a new nomination and go through the whole process again, the fact that you're that passionate about an academy education does count when they look at you the second time. If you know where you were weak (academics, test scores, athletics), you can spend the year beefing up that part of your record.

STEPS FOLLOWING ACCEPTANCE

When you click the button that says you accept your academy appointment, your candidate portal will open up with a whole new list of "to do" items. As before, they start red and your job is to turn them green. It's a pretty long list, so get on it as soon as possible.

Security Clearance

There are three basic levels of security clearance: Confidential, Secret, and Top Secret. (You'll often hear about security clearances "above Top Secret," but these normally refer to the depth of the background investigation or the types of information to which you have access. These kinds of clearances still fall under the category of Top Secret.)

As a cadet or midshipman, you will need to obtain a Secret security clearance. There are people at each academy who will give you full instructions, lead you through the process, and help resolve any issues you may have.

A Secret clearance isn't that difficult to obtain, but you do have to supply a lot of information. Standard Form 86 (SF 86), Questionnaire for National Security Positions, is the basic form for all levels of clearance. You can download a copy here: www.opm.gov/Forms/pdf_fill/sf86.pdf. The form is pretty intimidating, but you'll quickly notice that a lot of it doesn't apply to you.

You'll actually apply online, but you may find it very useful to fill out a paper copy first. Be sure to fill out the form accurately. Even if an omission or a misstatement is harmless in itself, the incorrect information can be a problem both now and down the line. Every time you renew or upgrade a clearance, your previous answers will be compared to your new answers. That's why it's a good idea to keep a paper copy of every SF 86 you complete throughout your entire military career (and civilian career if you stay in the secure world). Plus, gathering some of the information can be a bit of a pain, so you don't want to have to do it over again later.

Most of the information is pretty routine, such as previous addresses, schools attended, and jobs held. You'll be asked to supply contact information so your answers can be verified.

Some parts of the form may make you nervous. They'll ask about any foreign contacts, job problems, drug or alcohol abuse, and any encounters with law enforcement (whether or not you got arrested and whether or not you got convicted). If you've seen a counselor, they want to know about it. If you've already disclosed information to the academy or to DoDMERB and they've accepted you anyway, you're not going to be denied a security clearance because of them. Other information, such as seeing a counselor or traveling abroad, doesn't affect whether you get a clearance. It's just part of your security record.

In other words, don't worry. Remember that lying or withholding information is always more damaging than telling the truth. However, if you have any questions about what must be disclosed, discuss the matter with your academy contact.

Shoes and Boots

You'll receive your uniforms and other materials when you get there (they will ask you for measurements), but you'll need to buy boots and shoes early so you can break them in before reporting for duty. They'll send you a very specific list of acceptable brands, along with authorization to visit a Military Exchange store at a base near you. You can also get them on the Internet, but buy early enough so that if the first pair doesn't fit, you can exchange them. (We bought two pairs in different sizes and returned the pair that didn't fit.)

Money Issues

You'll need a bank account, a direct deposit authorization (remember, cadets and midshipmen get a salary, though much of that will go to purchasing books, computers, and other items), and you must put down an initial deposit (in our case, $2,000). If the initial deposit is a financial hardship, let your admission office know immediately.

Scholarships

What if you get a scholarship? If the scholarship is for tuition, room and board only, or if the scholarship is based on need rather than merit, you cannot accept it. After all, you're getting tuition, room and board, and a small salary already. If, on the other hand, the scholarship can be used for textbooks, uniforms, or other expenses, you *are* allowed to accept it. The awarding institution will have to send the check to the academy for deposit into your cadet or midshipman account. Each academy has instructions on how to handle this.

This doesn't apply to the Merchant Marine Academy, because it does charge tuition. They recommend you seek scholarships to defer educational costs and provide information here: www.usmma.edu/admissions/financial-aid/scholarships.

529 Plans

If your parents have been funding a 529 College Savings Plan to pay for your eventual college education, you may not need all the money they've saved up. While there's usually a tax penalty for taking out 529 Plan money for something other than college expenses, there are some exceptions, including receiving a full scholarship. You can also use 529 Plan money for expenses charged to your cadet or midshipman account (computers, uniforms, etc.). There are various arguments whether it's better to leave the money in or take it out; consult your tax advisor or financial planner for details.

Physical Training

Basic training for cadets and midshipmen is demanding, and the academies strongly recommend you follow a fitness program before going. They'll send you a recommended exercise program and schedule. That should be the minimum you do; more is better. Stamina is particularly important: run, run, run, and then run some more.

SPECIAL NOTE! If you're going to the Air Force Academy, remember that the campus ranges from 6,200 feet to 9,000 feet above sea level, high enough to experience symptoms of altitude sickness. If you come from lower elevations, be prepared for the shock of transition. For useful tips, the Academy suggests visiting Princeton University's Outdoor Action[6] site at www.princeton.edu/~oa/safety/altitude.shtml.

Parents

In addition to the usual trauma of launching your child into the great big world, you'll find quite a few adjustments you'll need to make, especially if you are not part of a military family yourself. Parents have dress codes for official events, are expected to control what information they post about their cadets and midshipmen on social media, and must understand the various rules about when and how you can contact your son or daughter.

You'll find it extremely valuable to join the regional chapter of your academy parents organization. From social events to parental reassurance to shared travel arrangements, you'll find that being part of a wider group will keep you closer to your cadet/midshipman and allow you to provide the support and resources that will make their academy years successful. You'll be given information on how to contact and join the parents club closest to you. These parents are a wealth of practical information. Make use of them.

Check the academy website for parent information and resources. In addition, appendix III lists some books and other material to help parents navigate the possibly unfamiliar environment of academy life.

REPORTING FOR DUTY

As an incoming cadet or midshipman, you'll report for basic training at the beginning of July, and you won't have any significant time off until Thanksgiving. This is often the most demanding and challenging part of your years at an academy, and it's important you start off on the right foot.

Travel Arrangements

You'll receive detailed information on arranging your travel to the academy, and you'll need to share your travel plans with them. Some of your travel expenses (but not your parents') are reimbursable as official government travel; be sure to keep receipts.

Packing Lists

You'll receive a detailed packing list. Pack exactly what they tell you, and *don't* bring anything else! After you complete your first summer's basic training, you're allowed a bit more flexibility in personal possessions, but the less you bring in the beginning, the better. On that first day, you'll be carrying all your possessions along with all the items you're issued, and you'll appreciate not having the extra weight.

While you can have personal electronics such as cell phones once the regular academic year begins, you won't have access to them during that first summer. If you can leave them behind and have them shipped to you later, that's easiest. Otherwise, you'll have to store them (along with anything else you're not permitted to have during basic training) until it's all over.

Reporting In

Your first day is a very intense experience, and your families can share in part of it. You will be given a reporting time, and you'd better say your goodbyes before you get there, because you have ninety seconds from the time you report to the time you need to walk through the door—time for one last hug, but that's it.

Wear nondescript clothes. Check hair regulations for men and women, and be ready. Males will have their heads shaved (don't do that in advance); while the rules for women are a bit more flexible, short and simple hair will make your life easier.

You'll spend the day going through one drill after another, from haircut to uniform measurement, to detailed instructions on what to do. There are online videos of the experience from a cadet/midshipman perspective; it's a good idea to watch them so you'll know what to expect and be ready. At the day's end, you'll be organized by company and conduct your first formal parade—and the next day, basic training begins in earnest.

Appendix III includes some videos of the reporting day experience for the various academies to give you some idea of your initial experience.

THE SHOCK OF TRANSITION AND THE MORALE CURVE

As you walk through the door on your first day to begin your adventure at a military service academy, this book comes to an end. Every person's experience is different. However, one thing is certain: you're going to have good and bad days.

No matter how much you prepare, no matter how much you read and study, no matter how many people you talk with, reality will inevitably turn out to be different from the way you expect.

While studying the performance of Peace Corps and VISTA volunteers, psychologist Dr. W. Walter Menninger identified what is now known as the Menninger Morale Curve[7], a picture of how most of us react to major life changes. For a positive change, from entering college to getting a job to getting married, we tend to start with an unrealistic view of the situation we're entering. After all, we haven't experienced it before, so everything is new. Excitement and morale are at their highest.

That unrealistic view quickly crumbles under pressure, new stimuli, and stress. A few people give up as soon as that first shock occurs. For most, reality sets in, and at the same time, morale crumbles. Somewhere between four and seven months into the process, morale hits a low point. "Why did I ever do this?"

In the same way that your initial high morale is unrealistic, the low point is equally unrealistic. You've been learning and adapting, which is very hard, but at this point you've actually moved quite a bit toward your eventual destination. Some people give up at this point, but most discover that once they've hit bottom, the morale curve starts to turn back up. At around the year mark, your morale is likely to be above the line, but not as high as it was in the beginning. It's more realistic, and that's good.

It's at this point you're truly able to assess where you are and where you want to be with some degree of objectivity and perspective. From here on out, you get to choose. If this is the road you truly want to be on, you now know how to navigate it. If it isn't, you can figure out what to do next.

There are two known strategies for helping people navigate the Morale Curve successfully. The first strategy is simple: you need to know it exists. When some people reach the low point, instead of realizing that this is normal and that everybody goes there sooner or later, they think there's something wrong with them, and that's not true.

The second thing that helps people through that low point is help from other people. The academies offer counseling and support—and what you're going through, they've seen many, many times. Nobody will think you're weak if you ask for help. Good friends and a good social support structure make a big difference, too.

You'll hear a lot of advice, much of it very good and some that's questionable at best. Take things one day at a time. This, too, shall pass. Everybody's got a weakness, and sooner or later, the academy will find yours.

Above all, remember that you're not in it by yourself. The line of cadets and midshipmen began long before you, and will continue long after you move on.

Good luck and best wishes.

— *** —

Appendix I

Laws Governing Appointments
to the Academies

UNITED STATES MILITARY ACADEMY

The Federal laws governing the United States Military Academy are spelled out in Title 10 of the U. S. Code, Chapter 403. The entire chapter can be found at http://www.law.cornell.edu/uscode/text/10/subtitle-B/part-III/chapter-403. The following sections apply to the admissions process:

10 U.S. Code § 4342 - Cadets: appointment; numbers, territorial distribution

(a) The authorized strength of the Corps of Cadets of the Academy (determined for any year as of the day before the last day of the academic year) is 4,400 or such lower number as may be prescribed by the Secretary of the Army under subsection (j). Subject to that limitation, cadets are selected as follows:

(1) 65 cadets selected in order of merit as established by competitive examinations from the children of members of the armed forces who were killed in action or died of, or have a service-connected disability rated at not less than 100 per centum resulting from, wounds or injuries received or diseases contracted in, or preexisting injury or disease aggravated by, active service, children of members who are in a "missing status" as defined in section 551 (2) of title 37, and children of civilian employees who are in "missing status" as defined in section 5561 (5) of title 5. The determination of the Department of Veterans Affairs as to service connection of the cause of death or disability, and the percentage at which the disability is rated, is binding upon the Secretary of the Army.

(2) Five cadets nominated at large by the Vice President or, if there is no Vice President, by the President pro tempore of the Senate.

(3) Ten cadets from each State, five of whom are nominated by each Senator from that State.

(4) Five cadets from each congressional district, nominated by the Representative from the district.

(5) Five cadets from the District of Columbia, nominated by the Delegate to the House of Representatives from the District of Columbia.

(6) Three cadets from the Virgin Islands, nominated by the Delegate in Congress from the Virgin Islands.

(7) Six cadets from Puerto Rico, five of whom are nominated by the Resident Commissioner from Puerto Rico and one who is a native of Puerto Rico nominated by the Governor of Puerto Rico.

(8) Three cadets from Guam, nominated by the Delegate in Congress from Guam.

(9) Two cadets from American Samoa, nominated by the Delegate in Congress from American Samoa.

(10) Two cadets from the Commonwealth of the Northern Mariana Islands, nominated by the Delegate in Congress from the commonwealth.

Each Senator, Representative, and Delegate in Congress, including the Resident Commissioner from Puerto Rico, is entitled to nominate 10 persons for each vacancy that is available to him under this section. Nominees may be submitted without ranking or with a principal candidate and 9 ranked or unranked alternates. Qualified nominees not selected for appointment under this subsection shall be considered qualified alternates for the purposes of selection under other provisions of this chapter.

(b) In addition, there may be appointed each year at the Academy cadets as follows:

(1) one hundred selected by the President from the children of members of an armed force who—

(A) are on active duty (other than for training) and who have served continuously on active duty for at least eight years;

(B) are, or who died while they were, retired with pay or granted retired or retainer pay;

(C) are serving as members of reserve components and are credited with at least eight years of service computed under section 12733 of this title; or

(D) would be, or who died while they would have been, entitled to retired pay under chapter 1223 of this title except for not having attained 60 years of age;

however, a person who is eligible for selection under paragraph (1) of subsection (a) may not be selected under this paragraph.

(2) 85 nominated by the Secretary of the Army from enlisted members of the Regular Army.

(3) 85 nominated by the Secretary of the Army from enlisted members of reserve components of the Army.

(4) 20 nominated by the Secretary of the Army, under regulations prescribed by him, from the honor graduates of schools designated as honor schools by the Department of the Army, the Department of the Navy, or the Department of the Air Force, and from members of the Reserve Officers' Training Corps.

(5) 150 selected by the Secretary of the Army in order of merit (prescribed pursuant to section 4343 of this title) from qualified alternates nominated by persons named in paragraphs (3) and (4) of subsection (a).

(c) The President may also appoint as cadets at the Academy children of persons who have been awarded the Medal of Honor for acts performed while in the armed forces.

(d) The Superintendent may nominate for appointment each year 50 persons from the country at large. Persons nominated under this paragraph may not displace any appointment authorized under paragraphs (2) through (9) of subsection (a) and may not cause the total strength of the Corps of Cadets to exceed the authorized number.

(e) If the annual quota of cadets under subsection (b)(1), (2), (3) is not filled, the Secretary may fill the vacancies by nominating for appointment other candidates from any of these sources who were found best qualified on examination for admission and not otherwise nominated.

(f) Each candidate for admission nominated under paragraphs (3) through (9) of subsection (a) must be domiciled in the State, or in the congressional district, from which he is nominated, or in the District of Columbia, Puerto Rico, American Samoa, Guam, or the Virgin Islands, if nominated from one of those places.

(g) The Secretary of the Army may limit the number of cadets authorized to be appointed under this section to the number that can be adequately accommodated at the Academy, as determined by the Secretary after consulting with the Committee on Armed Services of the Senate and the Committee on Armed Services of the House of Representatives, subject to the following:

(1) Cadets chargeable to each nominating authority named in subsection (a)(3) or (4) may not be limited to less than four.

(2) If the Secretary limits the number of appointments under subsection (a)(3) or (4), appointments under subsection (b)(1)–(4) are limited as follows:

(A) 27 appointments under subsection (b)(1);

(B) 27 appointments under subsection (b)(2);

(C) 27 appointments under subsection (b)(3); and

(D) 13 appointments under subsection (b)(4).

(3) If the Secretary limits the number of appointments under subsection (b)(5), appointments under subsection (b)(2)–(4) are limited as follows:

(A) 27 appointments under subsection (b)(2);

(B) 27 appointments under subsection (b)(3); and

(C) 13 appointments under subsection (b)(4).

(4) The limitations provided for in this subsection do not affect the operation of subsection (e).

(h) The Superintendent shall furnish to any Member of Congress, upon the written request of such Member, the name of the Congressman or other nominating authority responsible for the nomination of any named or identified person for appointment to the Academy.

(i) For purposes of the limitation in subsection (a) establishing the aggregate authorized strength of the Corps of Cadets, the Secretary of the Army may for any year permit a variance in that limitation by not more than one percent. In applying that limitation, and any such variance, the last day of an academic year shall be considered to be graduation day.

(j)

(1) Beginning with the 2003–2004 academic year, the Secretary of the Army may prescribe annual increases in the cadet strength limit in effect under subsection (a). For any academic year, any such increase shall be by no more than 100 cadets or such lesser number as applies under paragraph (3) for that year. Such annual increases may be prescribed until the cadet strength limit is 4,400.

(2) Any increase in the cadet strength limit under paragraph (1) with respect to an academic year shall be prescribed not later than the date on which the budget of the President is submitted to Congress under section 1105 of title 31 for the fiscal year beginning in the same year as the year in which that academic year begins. Whenever the Secretary prescribes such an increase, the Secretary shall submit to Congress a notice in writing of the increase. The notice shall state the amount of the increase in the cadet strength limit and the new cadet strength limit, as so increased, and the amount of the increase in Senior Army Reserve Officers' Training Corps enrollment under each of sections 2104 and 2107 of this title.

(3) The amount of an increase under paragraph (1) in the cadet strength limit for an academic year may not exceed the increase (if

any) for the preceding academic year in the total number of cadets enrolled in the Army Senior Reserve Officers' Training Corps program under chapter 103 of this title who have entered into an agreement under section 2104 or 2107 of this title.

(4) In this subsection, the term "cadet strength limit" means the authorized maximum strength of the Corps of Cadets of the Academy.

10 U.S. Code § 4343 - Cadets: appointment; to bring Corps to full strength

If it is determined that, upon the admission of a new class to the Academy, the number of cadets at the Academy will be below the authorized number, the Secretary of the Army may fill the vacancies by nominating additional cadets from qualified candidates designated as alternates and from other qualified candidates who competed for nomination and are recommended and found qualified by the Academic Board. At least three-fourths of those nominated under this section shall be selected from qualified alternates nominated by the persons named in paragraphs (2) through (8) of section 4342 (a) of this title, and the remainder from qualified candidates holding competitive nominations under any other provision of law. An appointment under this section is an additional appointment and is not in place of an appointment otherwise authorized by law.

10 U.S. Code § 4344 - Selection of persons from foreign countries

(a)

(1) The Secretary of the Army may permit not more than 60 persons at any one time from foreign countries to receive instruction at the Academy. Such persons shall be in addition to the authorized strength of the Corps of the Cadets of the Academy under section 4342 of this title.

(2) The Secretary of the Army, upon approval by the Secretary of Defense, shall determine the countries from which persons may be selected for appointment under this section and the number of persons that may be selected from each country. The Secretary of the Army may establish entrance qualifications and methods of competition for selection among individual applicants under this section and shall select those persons who will be permitted to receive instruction at the Academy under this section.

(3) In selecting persons to receive instruction under this section from among applicants from the countries approved under paragraph (2), the Secretary of the Army shall give a priority to persons who have a national service obligation to their countries upon graduation from the Academy.

(b)

(1) A person receiving instruction under this section is entitled to the pay, allowances, and emoluments of a cadet appointed from the United States, and from the same appropriations.

(2) Each foreign country from which a cadet is permitted to receive instruction at the Academy under this section shall reimburse the United States for the cost of providing such instruction, including the cost of pay, allowances, and emoluments provided under paragraph (1). The Secretary of the Army shall prescribe the rates for reimbursement under this paragraph, except that the reimbursement rates may not be less than the cost to the United States of providing such instruction, including pay, allowances, and emoluments, to a cadet appointed from the United States.

(3) The Secretary of Defense may waive, in whole or in part, the requirement for reimbursement of the cost of instruction for a cadet under paragraph (2). In the case of a partial waiver, the Secretary shall establish the amount waived.

(c)

(1) Except as the Secretary of the Army determines, a person receiving instruction under this section is subject to the same regulations governing admission, attendance, discipline, resignation, discharge, dismissal, and graduation as a cadet at the Academy appointed from the United States. The Secretary may prescribe regulations with respect to access to classified information by a person receiving instruction under this section that differ from the regulations that apply to a cadet at the Academy appointed from the United States.

(2) A person receiving instruction under this section is not entitled to an appointment in an armed force of the United States by reason of graduation from the Academy.

(d) A person receiving instruction under this section is not subject to section 4346 (d) of this title.

10 U.S. Code § 4346 - Cadets: requirements for admission

(a) To be eligible for admission to the Academy a candidate must be at least 17 years of age and must not have passed his twenty-third birthday on July 1 of the year in which he enters the Academy.

(b) To be admitted to the Academy, an appointee must show, by an examination held under regulations prescribed by the Secretary of the Army, that he is qualified in the subjects prescribed by the Secretary.

(c) A candidate designated as a principal or an alternate for appointment as a cadet shall appear for physical examination at a time and place designated by the Secretary.

(d) To be admitted to the Academy, an appointee must take and subscribe to the following oath—

"I, XXXXXXXXXXXX, do solemnly swear that I will support the Constitution of the United States, and bear true allegiance to the National Government; that I will maintain and defend the sovereignty of the United States, paramount to any and all allegiance, sovereignty, or fealty I may owe to any State or country whatsoever; and that I will at all times obey the legal orders of my superior officers, and the Uniform Code of Military Justice."

If a candidate for admission refuses to take this oath, his appointment is terminated.

10 U.S. Code § 4347 - Cadets; nominees: effect of redistricting of States

If as a result of redistricting a State the domicile of a cadet, or a nominee, nominated by a Representative falls within a congressional district other than that from which he was nominated, he is charged to the district in which his domicile so falls. For this purpose, the number of cadets otherwise authorized for that district is increased to include him. However, the number as so increased is reduced by one if he fails to become a cadet or when he is finally separated from the Academy.

10 U.S. Code § 4348 - Cadets: agreement to serve as officer

(a) Each cadet shall sign an agreement with respect to the cadet's length of service in the armed forces. The agreement shall provide that the cadet agrees to the following:

(1) That the cadet will complete the course of instruction at the Academy.

(2) That upon graduation from the Academy the cadet—

(A) will accept an appointment, if tendered, as a commissioned officer of the Regular Army or the Regular Air Force; and

(B) will serve on active duty for at least five years immediately after such appointment.

(3) That if an appointment described in paragraph (2) is not tendered or if the cadet is permitted to resign as a regular officer before completion of the commissioned service obligation of the cadet, the cadet—

(A) will accept an appointment as a commissioned officer as a Reserve for service in the Army Reserve or the Air Force Reserve; and

(B) will remain in that reserve component until completion of the commissioned service obligation of the cadet.

(4) That if an appointment described in paragraph (2) or (3) is tendered and the cadet participates in a program under section 2121 of this title, the cadet will fulfill any unserved obligation incurred under this section on active duty, regardless of the type of appointment held,

upon completion of, and in addition to, any service obligation incurred under section 2123 of this title for participation in such program.

(b)

(1) The Secretary of the Army may transfer to the Army Reserve, and may order to active duty for such period of time as the Secretary prescribes (but not to exceed four years), a cadet who breaches an agreement under subsection (a). The period of time for which a cadet is ordered to active duty under this paragraph may be determined without regard to section 651 (a) of this title.

(2) A cadet who is transferred to the Army Reserve under paragraph (1) shall be transferred in an appropriate enlisted grade or rating, as determined by the Secretary.

(3) For the purposes of paragraph (1), a cadet shall be considered to have breached an agreement under subsection (a) if the cadet is separated from the Academy under circumstances which the Secretary determines constitute a breach by the cadet of the cadet's agreement to complete the course of instruction at the Academy and accept an appointment as a commissioned officer upon graduation from the Academy.

(c) The Secretary of the Army shall prescribe regulations to carry out this section. Those regulations shall include—

(1) standards for determining what constitutes, for the purpose of subsection (b), a breach of an agreement under subsection (a);

(2) procedures for determining whether such a breach has occurred; and

(3) standards for determining the period of time for which a person may be ordered to serve on active duty under subsection (b).

(d) In this section, the term "commissioned service obligation," with respect to an officer who is a graduate of the Academy, means the period beginning on the date of the officer's appointment as a commissioned officer and ending on the sixth anniversary of such appointment or, at the discretion of the Secretary of Defense, any later date up to the eighth anniversary of such appointment.

(e)

(1) This section does not apply to a cadet who is not a citizen or national of the United States.

(2) In the case of a cadet who is a minor and who has parents or a guardian, the cadet may sign the agreement required by subsection (a) only with the consent of a parent or guardian.

(f) A cadet or former cadet who does not fulfill the terms of the agreement as specified under subsection (a), or the alternative obligation imposed under subsection (b), shall be subject to the repayment provisions of section 303a (e) of title 37.

UNITED STATES NAVAL ACADEMY

The Federal laws governing the United States Naval Academy are spelled out in Title 10 of the U. S. Code, Chapter 603. The entire chapter can be found at http://www.law.cornell.edu/uscode/text/10/subtitle-C/part-III/chapter-603. The following sections apply to the admissions process:

10 U.S. Code § 6954 - Midshipmen: number

(a) The authorized strength of the Brigade of Midshipmen (determined for any year as of the day before the last day of the academic year) is 4,400 or such lower number as may be prescribed by the Secretary of the Navy under subsection (h). Subject to that limitation, midshipmen are selected as follows:

(1) 65 selected in order of merit as established by competitive examination from the children of members of the armed forces who were killed in action or died of, or have a service-connected disability rated at not less than 100 per centum resulting from, wounds or injuries received or diseases contracted in, or preexisting injury or disease aggravated by, active service, children of members who are in a "missing status" as defined in section 551 (2) of title 37, and children of civilian employees who are in "missing status" as defined in section 5561 (5) of title 5. The determination of the Department of Veterans Affairs as to service connection of the cause of death or disability, and the percentage at which the disability is rated, is binding upon the Secretary of the Navy.

(2) Five nominated at large by the Vice President or, if there is no Vice President, by the President pro tempore of the Senate.

(3) Ten from each State, five of whom are nominated by each Senator from that State.

(4) Five nominated by each Representative in Congress.

(5) Five from the District of Columbia, nominated by the Delegate to the House of Representatives from the District of Columbia.

(6) Three from the Virgin Islands, nominated by the Delegate in Congress from the Virgin Islands.

(7) Six from Puerto Rico, five of whom are nominated by the Resident Commissioner from Puerto Rico and one who is a native of Puerto Rico nominated by the Governor of Puerto Rico.

(8) Three from Guam, nominated by the Delegate in Congress from Guam.

(9) Two from American Samoa, nominated by the Delegate in Congress from American Samoa.

(10) Two from the Commonwealth of the Northern Mariana Islands, nominated by the Delegate in Congress from the commonwealth.

Each Senator, Representative, and Delegate in Congress, including the Resident Commissioner from Puerto Rico, is entitled to nominate 10 persons for each vacancy that is available to him under this section. Nominees may be submitted without ranking or with a principal candidate and 9 ranked or unranked alternates. Qualified nominees not selected for appointment under this subsection shall be considered qualified alternates for the purposes of selection under other provisions of this chapter.

(b) In addition there may be appointed each year at the Academy midshipmen as follows:

(1) one hundred selected by the President from the children of members of an armed force who—

(A) are on active duty (other than for training) and who have served continuously on active duty for at least eight years;

(B) are, or who died while they were, retired with pay or granted retired or retainer pay;

(C) are serving as members of reserve components and are credited with at least eight years of service computed under section 12733 of this title; or

(D) would be, or who died while they would have been, entitled to retired pay under chapter 1223 of this title except for not having attained 60 years of age;

however, a person who is eligible for selection under paragraph (1) of subsection (a) may not be selected under this paragraph.

(2) 85 nominated by the Secretary of the Navy from enlisted members of the Regular Navy and the Regular Marine Corps.

(3) 85 nominated by the Secretary of the Navy from enlisted members of the Navy Reserve and the Marine Corps Reserve.

(4) 20 nominated by the Secretary of the Navy, under regulations prescribed by him, from the honor graduates of schools designated as honor schools by the Department of the Army, the Department of the Navy, or the Department of the Air Force, and from members of the Naval Reserve Officer's Training corps.

(5) 150 selected by the Secretary of the Navy in order of merit (prescribed pursuant to section 6956 of this title) from qualified alternates nominated by persons named in paragraphs (3) and (4) of subsection (a).

(c) The President may also appoint as midshipmen at the Academy children of persons who have been awarded the medal of honor for acts performed while in the armed forces.

(d) The Superintendent of the Naval Academy may nominate for appointment each year 50 persons from the country at large. Persons nominated under this paragraph may not displace any appointment authorized under paragraphs (2) through (9) of subsection (a) and may not cause the total strength of midshipmen at the Naval Academy to exceed the authorized number.

(e) The Secretary of the Navy may limit the number of midshipmen appointed under subsection (b)(5). When he does so, if the total number of midshipmen, upon admission of a new class at the Academy, will be more than 3,737, no appointments may be made under subsection (b)(2) or (3) of this section or section 6956 of this title.

(f) The Superintendent of the Naval Academy shall furnish to any Member of Congress, upon the written request of such Member, the name of the Congressman or other nominating authority responsible for the nomination of any named or identified person for appointment to the Academy.

(g) For purposes of the limitation in subsection (a) establishing the aggregate authorized strength of the Brigade of Midshipmen, the Secretary of the Navy may for any year permit a variance in that limitation by not more than one percent. In applying that limitation, and any such variance, the last day of an academic year shall be considered to be graduation day.

(h)

(1) Beginning with the 2003–2004 academic year, the Secretary of the Navy may prescribe annual increases in the midshipmen strength limit in effect under subsection (a). For any academic year, any such increase shall be by no more than 100 midshipmen or such lesser number as applies under paragraph (3) for that year. Such annual increases may be prescribed until the midshipmen strength limit is 4,400.

(2) Any increase in the midshipmen strength limit under paragraph (1) with respect to an academic year shall be prescribed not later than the date on which the budget of the President is submitted to Congress under section 1105 of title 31 for the fiscal year beginning in the same year as the year in which that academic year begins. Whenever the Secretary prescribes such an increase, the Secretary shall submit to Congress a notice in writing of the increase. The notice shall state the amount of the increase in the midshipmen strength limit and the new midshipmen strength limit, as so increased, and the amount of the increase in Senior Navy Reserve Officers' Training Corps enrollment under each of sections 2104 and 2107 of this title.

(3) The amount of an increase under paragraph (1) in the midshipmen strength limit for an academic year may not exceed the increase

(if any) for the preceding academic year in the total number of midshipmen enrolled in the Navy Senior Reserve Officers' Training Corps program under chapter 103 of this title who have entered into an agreement under section 2104 or 2107 of this title.

(4) In this subsection, the term "midshipmen strength limit" means the authorized maximum strength of the Brigade of Midshipmen.

10 U.S. Code § 6955 - Midshipmen: allotment upon redistricting of Congressional Districts

If as a result of redistricting a State the domicile of a midshipman, or a nominee, nominated by a Representative falls within a congressional district other than that from which he was nominated, he is charged to the district in which his domicile so falls. For this purpose, the number of midshipmen otherwise authorized for that district is increased to include him. However, the number as so increased is reduced by one if he fails to become a midshipman or when he is finally separated from the Naval Academy.

10 U.S. Code § 6956 - Midshipmen: nomination and selection to fill vacancies

(a) If the annual quota of midshipmen from—

(1) enlisted members of the Regular Navy and the Regular Marine Corps;

(2) enlisted members of the Navy Reserve and the Marine Corps Reserve; or

(3) at large by the President;

is not filled, the Secretary may fill the vacancies by nominating for appointment other candidates from any of these sources who were found best qualified on examination for admission and not otherwise nominated.

(b) If it is determined that, upon the admission of a new class to the Academy, the number of midshipmen at the Academy will be below the authorized number, the Secretary may fill the vacancies by nominating additional midshipmen from qualified candidates designated as alternates and from other qualified candidates who competed for nomination and are recommended and found qualified by the Academic Board. At least three-fourths of those nominated under this subsection shall be from qualified alternates under paragraphs (2) through (8) of section 6954 (a) of this title, and the remainder shall be from qualified candidates who competed for appointment under any other provision of law. An appointment of a nominee under this subsection is an additional appointment and is not in place of an appointment otherwise authorized by law.

(c) The failure of a member of a graduating class to complete the course with his class does not delay the appointment of his successor.

10 U.S. Code § 6957 - Selection of persons from foreign countries

(a)

(1) The Secretary of the Navy may permit not more than 60 persons at any one time from foreign countries to receive instruction at the Academy. Such persons shall be in addition to the authorized strength of the midshipmen under section 6954 of this title.

(2) The Secretary of the Navy, upon approval by the Secretary of Defense, shall determine the countries from which persons may be selected for appointment under this section and the number of persons that may be selected from each country. The Secretary of the Navy may establish entrance qualifications and methods of competition for selection among individual applicants under this section and shall select those persons who will be permitted to receive instruction at the Academy under this section.

(3) In selecting persons to receive instruction under this section from among applicants from the countries approved under paragraph (2), the Secretary of the Navy shall give a priority to persons who have a national service obligation to their countries upon graduation from the Academy.

(b)

(1) A person receiving instruction under this section is entitled to the pay, allowances, and emoluments of a midshipman appointed from the United States, and from the same appropriations.

(2) Each foreign country from which a midshipman is permitted to receive instruction at the Academy under this section shall reimburse the United States for the cost of providing such instruction, including the cost of pay, allowances, and emoluments provided under paragraph (1). The Secretary of the Navy shall prescribe the rates for reimbursement under this paragraph, except that the reimbursement rates may not be less than the cost to the United States of providing such instruction, including pay, allowances, and emoluments, to a midshipman appointed from the United States.

(3) The Secretary of Defense may waive, in whole or in part, the requirement for reimbursement of the cost of instruction for a midshipman under paragraph (2). In the case of a partial waiver, the Secretary shall establish the amount waived.

(c)

(1) Except as the Secretary of the Navy determines, a person receiving instruction under this section is subject to the same regulations

governing admission, attendance, discipline, resignation, discharge, dismissal, and graduation as a midshipman at the Academy appointed from the United States. The Secretary may prescribe regulations with respect to access to classified information by a person receiving instruction under this section that differ from the regulations that apply to a midshipman at the Academy appointed from the United States.

(2) A person receiving instruction under this section is not entitled to an appointment in an armed force of the United States by reason of graduation from the Academy.

(d) A person receiving instruction under this section is not subject to section 6958 (d) of this title.

10 U.S. Code § 6958 - Midshipmen: qualifications for admission

(a) Each candidate for admission to the Naval Academy—

(1) must be at least 17 years of age and must not have passed his twenty-third birthday on July 1 of the calendar year in which he enters the Academy; and

(2) shall be examined according to such regulations as the Secretary of the Navy prescribes, and if rejected at one examination may not be examined again for admission to the same class unless recommended by the Academic Board.

(b) Each candidate for admission nominated under clauses (3) through (9) of section 6954 (a) of this title must be domiciled in the State, or in the congressional district, from which he is nominated, or in the District of Columbia, Puerto Rico, American Samoa, Guam, or the Virgin Islands, if nominated from one of those places.

(c) Each candidate nominated under clause (2) or (3) of section 6954 (b) of this title—

(1) must be a citizen of the United States;

(2) must have passed the required physical examination; and

(3) shall be appointed in the order of merit from candidates who have, in competition with each other, passed the required mental examination.

(d) To be admitted to the Naval Academy, an appointee must take and subscribe to an oath prescribed by the Secretary of the Navy. If a candidate for admission refuses to take and subscribe to the prescribed oath, the candidate's appointment is terminated.

10 U.S. Code § 6959 - Midshipmen: agreement for length of service

(a) Each midshipman shall sign an agreement with respect to the midshipman's length of service in the armed forces. The agreement shall provide that the midshipman agrees to the following:

(1) That the midshipman will complete the course of instruction at the Naval Academy.

(2) That upon graduation from the Naval Academy the midshipman—

(A) will accept an appointment, if tendered, as a commissioned officer of the Regular Navy, the Regular Marine Corps, or the Regular Air Force; and

(B) will serve on active duty for at least five years immediately after such appointment.

(3) That if an appointment described in paragraph (2) is not tendered or if the midshipman is permitted to resign as a regular officer before completion of the commissioned service obligation of the midshipman, the midshipman—

(A) will accept an appointment as a commissioned officer in the Navy Reserve or the Marine Corps Reserve or as a Reserve in the Air Force for service in the Air Force Reserve; and

(B) will remain in that reserve component until completion of the commissioned service obligation of the midshipman.

(4) That if an appointment described in paragraph (2) or (3) is tendered and the midshipman participates in a program under section 2121 of this title, the midshipman will fulfill any unserved obligation incurred under this section on active duty, regardless of the type of appointment held, upon completion of, and in addition to, any service obligation incurred under section 2123 of this title for participation in such program.

(b)

(1) The Secretary of the Navy may transfer to the Navy Reserve or the Marine Corps Reserve, and may order to active duty for such period of time as the Secretary prescribes (but not to exceed four years), a midshipman who breaches an agreement under subsection (a). The period of time for which a midshipman is ordered to active duty under this paragraph may be determined without regard to section 651 (a) of this title.

(2) A midshipman who is transferred to the Navy Reserve or Marine Corps Reserve under paragraph (1) shall be transferred in an appropriate enlisted grade or rating, as determined by the Secretary.

(3) For the purposes of paragraph (1), a midshipman shall be considered to have breached an agreement under subsection (a) if the midshipman is separated from the Naval Academy under circumstances which the Secretary determines constitute a breach by the midshipman of the midshipman's agreement to complete the course of instruction at the Naval Academy and accept an appointment as a commissioned officer upon graduation from the Naval Academy.

(c) The Secretary of the Navy shall prescribe regulations to carry out this section. Those regulations shall include—

(1) standards for determining what constitutes, for the purpose of subsection (b), a breach of an agreement under subsection (a);

(2) procedures for determining whether such a breach has occurred; and

(3) standards for determining the period of time for which a person may be ordered to serve on active duty under subsection (b).

(d) In this section, "commissioned service obligation," with respect to an officer who is a graduate of the Academy, means the period beginning on the date of the officer's appointment as a commissioned officer and ending on the sixth anniversary of such appointment or, at the discretion of the Secretary of Defense, any later date up to the eighth anniversary of such appointment.

(e)

(1) This section does not apply to a midshipman who is not a citizen or national of the United States.

(2) In the case of a midshipman who is a minor and who has parents or a guardian, the midshipman may sign the agreement required by subsection (a) only with the consent of a parent or guardian.

(f) A midshipman or former midshipman who does not fulfill the terms of the agreement as specified under subsection (a), or the alternative obligation imposed under subsection (b), shall be subject to the repayment provisions of section 303a (e) of title 37.

UNITED STATES AIR FORCE ACADEMY

The Federal laws governing the United States Air Force Academy are spelled out in Title 10 of the U. S. Code, Chapter 903. The entire chapter can be found at http://www.law.cornell.edu/uscode/text/10/subtitle-D/part-III/chapter-903. The following sections apply to the admissions process:

10 U.S. Code § 9342 - Cadets: appointment; numbers, territorial distribution

(a) The authorized strength of Air Force Cadets of the Academy (determined for any year as of the day before the last day of the academic year) is 4,400 or such lower number as may be prescribed by the Secretary of the Air Force under subsection (j). Subject to that limitation, Air Force Cadets are selected as follows:

(1) 65 cadets selected in order of merit as established by competitive examination from the children of members of the armed forces who were killed in action or died of, or have a service-connected disability rated at not less than 100 per centum resulting from wounds

or injuries received or diseases contracted in, or preexisting injury or disease aggravated by, active service, children of members who are in a "missing status" as defined in section 551 (2) of title 37, and children of civilian employees who are in "missing status" as defined in section 5561 (5) of title 5. The determination of the Department of Veterans Affairs as to service connection of the cause of death or disability, and the percentage at which the disability is rated, is binding upon the Secretary of the Air Force.

(2) Five cadets nominated at large by the Vice President or, if there is no Vice President, by the President pro tempore of the Senate.

(3) Ten cadets from each State, five of whom are nominated by each Senator from that State.

(4) Five cadets from each congressional district, nominated by the Representative from the district.

(5) Five cadets from the District of Columbia, nominated by the Delegate to the House of Representatives from the District of Columbia.

(6) Three cadets from the Virgin Islands, nominated by the Delegate in Congress from the Virgin Islands.

(7) Six cadets from Puerto Rico, five of whom are nominated by the Resident Commissioner from Puerto Rico and one who is a native of Puerto Rico nominated by the Governor of Puerto Rico.

(8) Three cadets from Guam, nominated by the Delegate in Congress from Guam.

(9) Two cadets from American Samoa, nominated by the Delegate in Congress from American Samoa.

(10) Two cadets from the Commonwealth of the Northern Mariana Islands, nominated by the Delegate in Congress from the commonwealth.

Each Senator, Representative, and Delegate in Congress, including the Resident Commissioner from Puerto Rico, is entitled to nominate 10 persons for each vacancy that is available to him under this section. Nominees may be submitted without ranking or with a principal candidate and 9 ranked or unranked alternates. Qualified nominees not selected for appointment under this subsection shall be considered qualified alternates for the purposes of selection under other provisions of this chapter.

(b) In addition, there may be appointed each year at the Academy cadets as follows:

(1) one hundred selected by the President from the children of members of an armed force who—

(A) are on active duty (other than for training) and who have served continuously on active duty for at least eight years;

(B) are, or who died while they were, retired with pay or granted retired or retainer pay;

(C) are serving as members of reserve components and are credited with at least eight years of service computed under section 12733 of this title; or

(D) would be, or who died while they would have been, entitled to retired pay under chapter 1223 of this title except for not having attained 60 years of age;

however, a person who is eligible for selection under paragraph (1) of subsection (a) may not be selected under this paragraph.

(2) 85 nominated by the Secretary of the Air Force from enlisted members of the Regular Air Force.

(3) 85 nominated by the Secretary of the Air Force from enlisted members of reserve components of the Air Force.

(4) 20 nominated by the Secretary of the Air Force, under regulations prescribed by him, from the honor graduates of schools designated as honor schools by the Department of the Army, the Department of the Navy, or the Department of the Air Force, and from members of the Air Force Reserve Officers' Training Corps.

(5) 150 selected by the Secretary of the Air Force in order of merit (prescribed pursuant to section 9343 of this title) from qualified alternates nominated by persons named in paragraphs (3) and (4) of subsection (a).

(c) The President may also appoint as cadets at the Academy children of persons who have been awarded the Medal of Honor for acts performed while in the armed forces.

(d) The Superintendent may nominate for appointment each year 50 persons from the country at large. Persons nominated under this paragraph may not displace any appointment authorized under paragraphs (2) through (9) of subsection (a) and may not cause the total strength of Air Force Cadets to exceed the authorized number.

(e) If the annual quota of cadets under subsection (b)(1), (2), or (3) is not filled, the Secretary may fill the vacancies by nominating for appointment other candidates from any of these sources who were found best qualified on examination for admission and not otherwise nominated.

(f) Each candidate for admission nominated under paragraphs (3) through (9) of subsection (a) must be domiciled in the State, or in the congressional district, from which he is nominated, or in the District of Columbia, Puerto Rico, American Samoa, Guam, or the Virgin Islands, if nominated from one of those places.

(g) The Secretary of the Air Force may limit the number of cadets authorized to be appointed under this section to the number that can be adequately accommodated at the Academy as determined by the Secretary after consulting with the Committee on Armed Services of the Senate and the Committee on Armed Services of the House of Representatives, subject to the following:

(1) Cadets chargeable to each nominating authority named in subsection (a)(3) or (4) may not be limited to less than four.

(2) If the Secretary limits the number of appointments under subsection (a)(3) or (4), appointments under subsection (b)(1)–(4) are limited as follows:

(A) 27 appointments under subsection (b)(1);

(B) 27 appointments under subsection (b)(2);

(C) 27 appointments under subsection (b)(3); and

(D) 13 appointments under subsection (b)(4).

(3) If the Secretary limits the number of appointments under subsection (b)(5), appointments under subsection (b)(2)–(4) are limited as follows:

(A) 27 appointments under subsection (b)(2);

(B) 27 appointments under subsection (b)(3); and

(C) 13 appointments under subsection (b)(4).

(4) The limitations provided for in this subsection do not affect the operation of subsection (e).

(h) The Superintendent shall furnish to any Member of Congress, upon the written request of such Member, the name of the Congressman or other nominating authority responsible for the nomination of any named or identified person for appointment to the Academy.

(i) For purposes of the limitation in subsection (a) establishing the aggregate authorized strength of Air Force Cadets, the Secretary of the Air Force may for any year permit a variance in that limitation by not more than one percent. In applying that limitation, and any such variance, the last day of an academic year shall be considered to be graduation day.

(j)

(1) Beginning with the 2003–2004 academic year, the Secretary of the Air Force may prescribe annual increases in the cadet strength limit in effect under subsection (a). For any academic year, any such increase shall be by no more than 100 cadets or such lesser number as applies under paragraph (3) for that year. Such annual increases may be prescribed until the cadet strength limit is 4,400.

(2) Any increase in the cadet strength limit under paragraph (1) with respect to an academic year shall be prescribed not later than the

date on which the budget of the President is submitted to Congress under sections 1105 of title 31 for the fiscal year beginning in the same year as the year in which that academic year begins. Whenever the Secretary prescribes such an increase, the Secretary shall submit to Congress a notice in writing of the increase. The notice shall state the amount of the increase in the cadet strength limit and the new cadet strength limit, as so increased, and the amount of the increase in Senior Air Force Reserve Officers' Training Corps enrollment under each of sections 2104 and 2107 of this title.

(3) The amount of an increase under paragraph (1) in the cadet strength limit for an academic year may not exceed the increase (if any) for the preceding academic year in the total number of cadets enrolled in the Air Force Senior Reserve Officers' Training Corps program under chapter 103 of this title who have entered into an agreement under section 2104 or 2107 of this title.

(4) In this subsection, the term "cadet strength limit" means the authorized maximum strength of Air Force Cadets of the Academy.

10 U.S. Code § 9343 - Cadets: appointment; to bring to full strength

If it is determined that, upon the admission of a new class to the Academy, the number of cadets at the Academy will be below the authorized number, the Secretary of the Air Force may fill the vacancies by nominating additional cadets from qualified candidates designated as alternates and from other qualified candidates who competed for nomination and are recommended and found qualified by the Academy Board. At least three-fourths of those nominated under this section shall be selected from qualified alternates nominated by the persons named in paragraphs (2) through (8) of section 9342 (a) of this title, and the remainder from qualified candidates holding competitive nominations under any other provision of law. An appointment under this section is an additional appointment and is not in place of an appointment otherwise authorized by law.

10 U.S. Code § 9344 - Selection of persons from foreign countries

(a)

(1) The Secretary of the Air Force may permit not more than 60 persons at any one time from foreign countries to receive instruction at the Academy. Such persons shall be in addition to the authorized strength of the Air Force Cadets of the Academy under section 9342 of this title.

(2) The Secretary of the Air Force, upon approval by the Secretary of Defense, shall determine the countries from which persons may be selected for appointment under this section and the number of persons

that may be selected from each country. The Secretary of the Air Force may establish entrance qualifications and methods of competition for selection among individual applicants under this section and shall select those persons who will be permitted to receive instruction at the Academy under this section.

(3) In selecting persons to receive instruction under this section from among applicants from the countries approved under paragraph (2), the Secretary of the Air Force shall give a priority to persons who have a national service obligation to their countries upon graduation from the Academy.

(b)

(1) A person receiving instruction under this section is entitled to the pay, allowances, and emoluments of a cadet appointed from the United States, and from the same appropriations.

(2) Each foreign country from which a cadet is permitted to receive instruction at the Academy under this section shall reimburse the United States for the cost of providing such instruction, including the cost of pay, allowances, and emoluments provided under paragraph (1). The Secretary of the Air Force shall prescribe the rates for reimbursement under this paragraph, except that the reimbursement rates may not be less than the cost to the United States of providing such instruction, including pay, allowances, and emoluments, to a cadet appointed from the United States.

(3) The Secretary of Defense may waive, in whole or in part, the requirement for reimbursement of the cost of instruction for a cadet under paragraph (2). In the case of a partial waiver, the Secretary shall establish the amount waived.

(c)

(1) Except as the Secretary of the Air Force determines, a person receiving instruction under this section is subject to the same regulations governing admission, attendance, discipline, resignation, discharge, dismissal, and graduation as a cadet at the Academy appointed from the United States. The Secretary may prescribe regulations with respect to access to classified information by a person receiving instruction under this section that differ from the regulations that apply to a cadet at the Academy appointed from the United States.

(2) A person receiving instruction under this section is not entitled to an appointment in an armed force of the United States by reason of graduation from the Academy.

(d) A person receiving instruction under this section is not subject to section 9346 (d) of this title.

10 U.S. Code § 9346 - Cadets: requirements for admission

(a) To be eligible for admission to the Academy a candidate must be at least 17 years of age and must not have passed his twenty-third birthday on July 1 of the year in which he enters the Academy.

(b) To be admitted to the Academy, an appointee must show, by an examination held under regulations prescribed by the Secretary of the Air Force, that he is qualified in the subjects prescribed by the Secretary.

(c) A candidate designated as a principal or an alternate for appointment as a cadet shall appear for physical examination at a time and place designated by the Secretary.

(d) To be admitted to the Academy, an appointee must take and subscribe to an oath prescribed by the Secretary of the Air Force. If a candidate for admission refuses to take and subscribe to the prescribed oath, his appointment is terminated.

10 U.S. Code § 9347 - Cadets; nominees: effect of redistricting of States

If as a result of redistricting a State the domicile of a cadet, or a nominee, nominated by a Representative falls within a congressional district other than that from which he was nominated, he is charged to the district in which his domicile so falls. For this purpose, the number of cadets otherwise authorized for that district is increased to include him. However, the number as so increased is reduced by one if he fails to become a cadet or when he is finally separated from the Academy.

10 U.S. Code § 9348 - Cadets: agreement to serve as officer

(a) Each cadet shall sign an agreement with respect to the cadet's length of service in the armed forces. The agreement shall provide that the cadet agrees to the following:

(1) That the cadet will complete the course of instruction at the Academy.

(2) That upon graduation from the Academy the cadet—

(A) will accept an appointment, if tendered, as a commissioned officer of the Regular Air Force; and

(B) will serve on active duty for at least five years immediately after such appointment.

(3) That if an appointment described in paragraph (2) is not tendered or if the cadet is permitted to resign as a regular officer before completion of the commissioned service obligation of the cadet, the cadet—

(A) will accept an appointment as a commissioned officer as a Reserve in the Air Force for service in the Air Force Reserve; and

(B) will remain in that reserve component until completion of the commissioned service obligation of the cadet.

(4) That if an appointment described in paragraph (2) or (3) is tendered and the cadet participates in a program under section 2121 of this title, the cadet will fulfill any unserved obligation incurred under this section on active duty, regardless of the type of appointment held, upon completion of, and in addition to, any service obligation incurred under section 2123 of this title for participation in such program.

(b)

(1) The Secretary of the Air Force may transfer to the Air Force Reserve, and may order to active duty for such period of time as the Secretary prescribes (but not to exceed four years), a cadet who breaches an agreement under subsection (a). The period of time for which a cadet is ordered to active duty under this paragraph may be determined without regard to section 651 (a) of this title.

(2) A cadet who is transferred to the Air Force Reserve under paragraph (1) shall be transferred in an appropriate enlisted grade or rating, as determined by the Secretary.

(3) For the purposes of paragraph (1), a cadet shall be considered to have breached an agreement under subsection (a) if the cadet is separated from the Academy under circumstances which the Secretary determines constitute a breach by the cadet of the cadet's agreement to complete the course of instruction at the Academy and accept an appointment as a commissioned officer upon graduation from the Academy.

(c) The Secretary of the Air Force shall prescribe regulations to carry out this section. Those regulations shall include—

(1) standards for determining what constitutes, for the purpose of subsection (b), a breach of an agreement under subsection (a);

(2) procedures for determining whether such a breach has occurred; and

(3) standards for determining the period of time for which a person may be ordered to serve on active duty under subsection(b).

(d) In this section, the term "commissioned service obligation," with respect to an officer who is a graduate of the Academy, means the period beginning on the date of the officer's appointment as a commissioned officer and ending on the sixth anniversary of such appointment or, at the discretion of the Secretary of Defense, any later date up to the eighth anniversary of such appointment.

(e)

(1) This section does not apply to a cadet who is not a citizen or national of the United States.

(2) In the case of a cadet who is a minor and who has parents or a guardian, the cadet may sign the agreement required by subsection (a) only with the consent of a parent or guardian.

(f) A cadet or former cadet who does not fulfill the terms of the agreement as specified under subsection (a), or the alternative obligation imposed under subsection (b), shall be subject to the repayment provisions of section 303a (e) of title 37.

UNITED STATES COAST GUARD ACADEMY

The Federal laws governing the United States Coast Guard Academy are spelled out in Title 14 of the U. S. Code, Chapter 9. The entire chapter can be found at http://www.law.cornell.edu/uscode/text/14/part-I/chapter-9. The following sections apply to the admissions process:

14 U.S. Code § 182 - Cadets; number, appointment, obligation to serve

(a) The number of cadets appointed annually to the Academy shall be as determined by the Secretary but the number appointed in any one year shall not exceed six hundred. Appointments to cadetships shall be made under regulations prescribed by the Secretary, who shall determine age limits, methods of selection of applicants, term of service as a cadet before graduation, and all other matters affecting such appointments. In the administration of this chapter, the Secretary shall take such action as may be necessary and appropriate to insure that female individuals shall be eligible for appointment and admission to the Coast Guard Academy, and that the relevant standards required for appointment, admission, training, graduation, and commissioning of female individuals shall be the same as those required for male individuals, except for those minimum essential adjustments in such standards required because of physiological differences between male and female individuals. The Secretary may summarily dismiss from the Coast Guard any cadet who, during his cadetship, is found unsatisfactory in either studies or conduct, or may be deemed not adapted for a career in the Coast Guard. Cadets shall be subject to rules governing discipline prescribed by the Commandant.

(b) Each cadet shall sign an agreement with respect to the cadet's length of service in the Coast Guard. The agreement shall provide that the cadet agrees to the following:

(1) That the cadet will complete the course of instruction at the Coast Guard Academy.

(2) That upon graduation from the Coast Guard Academy the cadet—

(A) will accept an appointment, if tendered, as a commissioned officer of the Coast Guard; and

(B) will serve on active duty for at least five years immediately after such appointment.

(3) That if an appointment described in paragraph (2) is not tendered or if the cadet is permitted to resign as a regular officer before the completion of the commissioned service obligation of the cadet, the cadet—

(A) will accept an appointment as a commissioned officer in the Coast Guard Reserve; and

(B) will remain in that reserve component until completion of the commissioned service obligation of the cadet.

(c)

(1) The Secretary may transfer to the Coast Guard Reserve, and may order to active duty for such period of time as the Secretary prescribes (but not to exceed four years), a cadet who breaches an agreement under subsection (b). The period of time for which a cadet is ordered to active duty under this paragraph may be determined without regard to section 651 (a) of title 10.

(2) A cadet who is transferred to the Coast Guard Reserve under paragraph (1) shall be transferred in an appropriate enlisted grade or rating, as determined by the Secretary.

(3) For the purposes of paragraph (1), a cadet shall be considered to have breached an agreement under subsection (b) if the cadet is separated from the Coast Guard Academy under circumstances which the Secretary determines constitute a breach by the cadet of the cadet's agreement to complete the course of instruction at the Coast Guard Academy and accept an appointment as a commissioned officer upon graduation from the Coast Guard Academy.

(d) The Secretary shall prescribe regulations to carry out this section. Those regulations shall include—

(1) standards for determining what constitutes, for the purpose of subsection (c), a breach of an agreement under subsection (b);

(2) procedures for determining whether such a breach has occurred; and

(3) standards for determining the period of time for which a person may be ordered to serve on active duty under subsection (c).

(e) In this section, "commissioned service obligation," with respect to an officer who is a graduate of the Academy, means the period beginning on the date of the officer's appointment as a commissioned officer and ending on the sixth anniversary of such appointment or, at the discretion of the Secretary, any later date up to the eighth anniversary of such appointment.

(f)

(1) This section does not apply to a cadet who is not a citizen or national of the United States.

(2) In the case of a cadet who is a minor and who has parents or a guardian, the cadet may sign the agreement required by subsection (b) only with the consent of the parent or guardian.

(g) A cadet or former cadet who does not fulfill the terms of the obligation to serve as specified under section (b), or the alternative obligation imposed under subsection (c), shall be subject to the repayment provisions of section 303a (e) of title 37.

14 U.S. Code § 195 - Admission of foreign nationals for instruction; restrictions; conditions

(a) A foreign national may not receive instruction at the Academy except as authorized by this section.

(b) The President may designate not more than 36 foreign nationals whom the Secretary may permit to receive instruction at the Academy.

(c) A foreign national receiving instruction under this section is entitled to the same pay, allowances, and emoluments, to be paid from the same appropriations, as a cadet appointed pursuant to section 182 of this title. A foreign national may receive instruction under this section only if his country agrees in advance to reimburse the United States, at a rate determined by the Secretary, for the cost of providing such instruction, including pay, allowances, and emoluments, unless a waiver therefrom has been granted to that country by the Secretary. Funds received by the Secretary for this purpose shall be credited to the appropriations bearing the cost thereof, and may be apportioned between fiscal years.

(d) A foreign national receiving instruction under this section is—

(1) not entitled to any appointment in the Coast Guard by reason of his graduation from the Academy; and

(2) subject to those regulations applicable to the Academy governing admission, attendance, discipline, resignation, discharge, dismissal, and graduation, except as may otherwise be prescribed by the Secretary.

UNITED STATES MERCHANT MARINE ACADEMY

The Federal laws governing the United States Merchant Marine Academy are spelled out in Title 46 of the U. S. Code, Chapter 513. The entire chapter can be found at http://www.law.cornell.edu/uscode/text/46/subtitle-V/part-B/chapter-513. The following sections apply to the admissions process:

46 U.S. Code § 51302 - Nomination and competitive appointment of cadets

(a) **Requirements.**— An individual may be nominated for a competitive appointment as a cadet at the United States Merchant Marine Academy only if the individual—

(1) is a citizen or national of the United States; and

(2) meets the minimum requirements that the Secretary of Transportation shall establish.

(b) **Nominators.**— Nominations for competitive appointments for the positions allocated under subsection (c) may be made as follows:

(1) A Senator may nominate residents of the State represented by that Senator.

(2) A Member of the House of Representatives may nominate residents of the State in which the congressional district represented by that Member is located.

(3) A Delegate to the House of Representatives from the District of Columbia, the Virgin Islands, Guam, the Northern Mariana Islands, or American Samoa may nominate residents of the jurisdiction represented by that Delegate.

(4) The Resident Commissioner to the United States from Puerto Rico may nominate residents of Puerto Rico.

(5) The Panama Canal Commission may nominate—

(A) residents, or sons or daughters of residents, of an area or installation in Panama and made available to the United States under the Panama Canal Treaty of 1977, the agreements relating to and implementing that Treaty, signed September 7, 1977, and the Agreement Between the United States of America and the Republic of Panama Concerning Air Traffic Control and Related Services, concluded January 8, 1979; and

(B) sons or daughters of personnel of the United States Government and the Panama Canal Commission residing in Panama.

(c) **Allocation of Positions.**— Positions for competitive appointments shall be allocated each year as follows:

(1) Positions shall be allocated for residents of each State nominated by the Members of Congress from that State in proportion to the representation in Congress from that State.

(2) Four positions shall be allocated for residents of the District of Columbia nominated by the Delegate to the House of Representatives from the District of Columbia.

(3) One position each shall be allocated for residents of the Virgin Islands, Guam, and American Samoa nominated by the Delegates to the House of Representatives from the Virgin Islands, Guam, and American Samoa, respectively.

(4) One position shall be allocated for a resident of Puerto Rico nominated by the Resident Commissioner to the United States from Puerto Rico.

(5) One position shall be allocated for a resident of the Northern Mariana Islands nominated by the Governor of the Northern Mariana Islands.

(6) Two positions shall be allocated for individuals nominated by the Panama Canal Commission.

(d) Competitive System for Appointment.—

(1) **Establishment of system.**— The Secretary shall establish a competitive system for selecting individuals nominated under subsection (b) to fill the positions allocated under subsection (c). The system must determine the relative merit of each individual based on competitive examinations, an assessment of the individual's academic background, and other effective indicators of motivation and probability of successful completion of training at the Academy.

(2) **Appointments by jurisdiction.**— The Secretary shall appoint individuals to fill the positions allocated under subsection (c) for each jurisdiction in the order of merit of the individuals nominated from that jurisdiction.

(3) **Remaining unfilled positions.**— If positions remain unfilled after the appointments are made under paragraph (2), the Secretary shall appoint individuals to fill the positions in the order of merit of the remaining individuals nominated from all jurisdictions.

46 U.S. Code § 51303 - Non-competitive appointments

The Secretary of Transportation may appoint each year without competition as cadets at the United States Merchant Marine Academy not more than 40 qualified individuals with qualities the Secretary considers to be of special value to the Academy. In making these appointments, the Secretary shall try to achieve a national demographic balance at the Academy.

46 U.S. Code § 51304 - Additional appointments from particular areas

(a) **Other Countries in Western Hemisphere.**— The President may appoint individuals from countries in the Western Hemisphere other than the United States to receive instruction at the United States Merchant Marine Academy. Not more than 12 individuals may receive instruction under this subsection at the same time, and not more than

2 individuals from the same country may receive instruction under this subsection at the same time.

(b) Other Countries Generally.—

(1) **Appointment**.— The Secretary of Transportation, with the approval of the Secretary of State, may appoint individuals from countries other than the United States to receive instruction at the Academy. Not more than 30 individuals may receive instruction under this subsection at the same time.

(2) **Reimbursement**.— The Secretary of Transportation shall ensure that the country from which an individual comes under this subsection will reimburse the Secretary for the cost (as determined by the Secretary) of the instruction and allowances received by the individual.

(c) Panama.—

(1) **Appointment**.— The Secretary of Transportation, with the approval of the Secretary of State, may appoint individuals from Panama to receive instruction at the Academy. Individuals appointed under this subsection are in addition to those appointed under any other provision of this chapter.

(2) **Reimbursement**.— The Secretary of Transportation shall be reimbursed for the cost (as determined by the Secretary) of the instruction and allowances received by an individual appointed under this subsection.

(d) **Allowances and Regulations**.— Individuals receiving instruction under this section are entitled to the same allowances and are subject to the same regulations on admission, attendance, discipline, resignation, discharge, dismissal, and graduation, as cadets at the Academy appointed from the United States.

46 U.S. Code § 51305 - Prohibited basis for appointment

Preference may not be given to an individual for appointment as a cadet at the United States Merchant Marine Academy because one or more members of the individual's immediate family are alumni of the Academy.

46 U.S. Code § 51306 - Cadet commitment agreements

(a) **Agreement Requirements**.— A citizen of the United States appointed as a cadet at the United States Merchant Marine Academy must sign, as a condition of the appointment, an agreement to—

(1) complete the course of instruction at the Academy;

(2) fulfill the requirements for a license as an officer in the merchant marine of the United States before graduation from the Academy;

(3) maintain a valid license as an officer in the merchant marine of the United States for at least 6 years after graduation from the Acad-

emy, accompanied by the appropriate national and international endorsements and certification required by the Coast Guard for service aboard vessels on domestic and international voyages;

(4) apply for, and accept if tendered, an appointment as a commissioned officer in the Navy Reserve (including the Merchant Marine Reserve, Navy Reserve), the Coast Guard Reserve, or any other reserve unit of an armed force of the United States, and, if tendered the appointment, to serve for at least 6 years after graduation from the Academy;

(5) serve the foreign and domestic commerce and the national defense of the United States for at least 5 years after graduation from the Academy—

(A) as a merchant marine officer on a documented vessel or a vessel owned and operated by the United States Government or by a State;

(B) as an employee in a United States maritime-related industry, profession, or marine science (as determined by the Secretary of Transportation), if the Secretary determines that service under subparagraph (A) is not available to the individual;

(C) as a commissioned officer on active duty in an armed force of the United States, as a commissioned officer in the National Oceanic and Atmospheric Administration, or in other maritime-related Federal employment which serves the national security interests of the United States, as determined by the Secretary; or

(D) by a combination of the service alternatives referred to in subparagraphs (A)–(C); and

(6) report to the Secretary on compliance with this subsection.

(b) Failure To Complete Course of Instruction.—

(1) **Active duty.**— If the Secretary of Transportation determines that an individual who has attended the Academy for at least 2 years has failed to fulfill the part of the agreement described in subsection (a) (1), the individual may be ordered by the Secretary of Defense to serve on active duty in one of the armed forces of the United States for a period of not more than 2 years. In cases of hardship as determined by the Secretary of Transportation, the Secretary of Transportation may waive this paragraph in whole or in part.

(2) **Recovery of cost.**— If the Secretary of Defense is unable or unwilling to order an individual to serve on active duty under paragraph (1), or if the Secretary of Transportation determines that reimbursement of the cost of education provided would better serve the interests of the United States, the Secretary of Transportation may recover from the individual the cost of education provided by the Government.

(c) Failure To Carry Out Other Requirements.—

(1) **Active duty.**— If the Secretary of Transportation determines that an individual has failed to fulfill any part of the agreement de-

scribed in subsection (a)(2)–(6), the individual may be ordered to serve on active duty for a period of at least 3 years but not more than the unexpired period (as determined by the Secretary) of the service required by subsection (a)(5). The Secretary of Transportation, in consultation with the Secretary of Defense, shall determine in which service the individual shall serve. In cases of hardship as determined by the Secretary of Transportation, the Secretary of Transportation may waive this paragraph in whole or in part.

(2) **Recovery of cost.**— If the Secretary of Defense is unable or unwilling to order an individual to serve on active duty under paragraph (1), or if the Secretary of Transportation determines that reimbursement of the cost of education provided would better serve the interests of the United States, the Secretary of Transportation may recover from the individual the cost of education provided. The Secretary may reduce the amount to be recovered to reflect partial performance of service obligations and other factors the Secretary determines merit a reduction.

(d) **Actions To Recover Cost.**— To aid in the recovery of the cost of education provided by the Government under a commitment agreement under this section, the Secretary of Transportation may—

(1) request the Attorney General to bring a civil action against the individual; and

(2) make use of the Federal debt collection procedures in chapter 176 of title 28 or other applicable administrative remedies.

(e) **Alternative Service.**—

(1) **Service as commissioned officer.**— An individual who, for the 5-year period following graduation from the Academy, serves as a commissioned officer on active duty in an armed force of the United States or as a commissioned officer of the National Oceanic and Atmospheric Administration or the Public Health Service shall be excused from the requirements of paragraphs (3) through (5) of subsection (a).

(2) **Modification or waiver.**— The Secretary may modify or waive any of the terms and conditions set forth in subsection (a) through the imposition of alternative service requirements.

(f) **Service Obligation Performance Reporting Requirement.**—

(1) **In general.**— Subject to any otherwise applicable restrictions on disclosure in section 552a of title 5, the Secretary of Defense, the Secretary of the department in which the Coast Guard is operating, the Administrator of the National Oceanic and Atmospheric Administration, and the Surgeon General of the Public Health Service—

(A) shall report the status of obligated service of an individual graduate of the Academy upon request of the Secretary; and

(B) may, in their discretion, notify the Secretary of any failure of the graduate to perform the graduate's duties, either on active duty or in the Ready Reserve component of their respective service, or as a commissioned officer of the National Oceanic and Atmospheric Administration or the Public Health Service, respectively.

(2) **Information to be provided.**— A report or notice under paragraph (1) shall identify any graduate determined to have failed to comply with service obligation requirements and provide all required information as to why such graduate failed to comply.

(3) **Considered as in default.**— Upon receipt of such a report or notice, such graduate may be considered to be in default of the graduate's service obligations by the Secretary, and subject to all remedies the Secretary may have with respect to such a default.

46 U.S. Code § 51310 - Deferment of service obligation under cadet commitment agreements

The Secretary of Transportation may defer the service commitment of an individual under section 51306 (a)(5) of this title (as specified in the cadet commitment agreement) for not more than 2 years if the individual is engaged in a graduate course of study approved by the Secretary. However, deferment of service as a commissioned officer under section 51306 (a)(5) must be approved by the Secretary of the military department that has jurisdiction over the service or by the Secretary of Commerce for service with the National Oceanic and Atmospheric Administration.

46 U.S. Code § 51311 - Midshipman status in the Navy Reserve

(a) **Application Requirement.**— Before being appointed as a cadet at the United States Merchant Marine Academy, a citizen of the United States must agree to apply for midshipman status in the Navy Reserve (including the Merchant Marine Reserve, Navy Reserve).

(b) Appointment.—

(1) **In general.**— A citizen of the United States appointed as a cadet at the Academy shall be appointed by the Secretary of the Navy as a midshipman in the Navy Reserve (including the Merchant Marine Reserve, Navy Reserve).

(2) **Rights and privileges.**— The Secretary of the Navy shall provide for cadets of the Academy who are midshipmen in the United States Navy Reserve to be—

(A) issued an identification card (referred to as a "military ID card"); and

(B) entitled to all rights and privileges in accordance with the same eligibility criteria as apply to other members of the Ready Reserve of the reserve components of the armed forces.

(3) **Coordination.**— The Secretary of the Navy shall carry out paragraphs (1) and (2) in coordination with the Secretary of Transportation.

Appendix II

Class Profiles

In determining how competitive you are for an academy appointment, it's useful to see how you measure up against the class averages. If you have some years to go before you apply, these class averages can help you set goals.

In the following pages, you'll find class profiles from each of the academies, current at the time of writing. (As new profiles are released, they'll be added to the supplemental PDF referenced in "How to Use This Book.") The information provided is not consistent because each academy chooses to present the data its own way.

If you don't score at the top by every measure, don't worry. Nobody is equally outstanding at everything. If you're strong in a few areas, you can be below average in others and still be competitive. However, the academies favor well-rounded candidates. Sometimes it can be more valuable to work on your weaknesses than the areas where you're already strong.

SPECIAL NOTE! Don't limit yourself to your own choice of academy when reviewing this information. In general, if one academy lists it, all the academies care about it. For example, the Naval Academy profile is the only one to list "Hardship and Adverse Life Experience" as a category, but all of the academies take that into account as a factor when evaluating candidates (see chapter 6).

Table A-1.   United States Military Academy Class Profile

Volume of Applicants	Men	Women	Total
Applicant Files Started/ Percent of Total	11,027/80%	2,800/20%	13,827/100%
Nominated/Percent	3,423/31%	697/25%	4,120/30%
Qualified/Percent	1,974/18%	386/14%	2,360/17%
Admitted/Percent	1,041/9%	216/8%	1,257/9%

		TEST SCORES			
ACT	English	Math	Science	Reading	Writing
Mean Score	29	29	28	30	28
SAT	Reading	Math	Writing		
Mean Score	627	645	608		
Class Rank	Top 20%	Second 20%	Third 20%	Fourth 20%	Bottom 20%
High School	70%	20%	9%	2%	0%

HONORS AND ACCOMPLISHMENTS (from admitted class of 1,257)

ACADEMIC	Valedictorian	Salutatorian	National Merit Scholar	National Honor Society
High School	92	49	198	731

LEADERSHIP	Class/Student Body President	Newspaper Editor/Staff	Yearbook Editor/ Co-Editor	Boys/Girls State	Scouting	Eagle/ Gold
	221	121	103	234	410	169

ATHLETICS	Team Captain	Varsity Letter	Total Participation
	771	1087	1156
OTHER	Debate	Drama	Prior Service/Combat Veteran
	161	120	23

Table A-2.   United States Naval Academy Class Profile

SAT Scores	Verbal	Math
Middle 50th Percentile	600–650	630–680

Class Composition	
Varsity Athletics	90%
Community Service	91%
Dramatics, Public Speaking, or Debating	67%
Captain/Co-Captain of Sports Team	69%
Student Body Leader	69%
National Honor Society	66%
Church Group	52%
Tutoring	46%
Work Experience (>10 hours/week)	16%
Music (Band, Chorus, etc.)	30%
ROTC/JROTC/Sea Cadets/Civil Air Patrol	17%
Hardship or Adverse Life Experience	21%
School Publication	11%

Table A-3.   United States Coast Guard Academy Class Profile

ACADEMICS

Class Rank	Top 5%	Top 10%	Top 25%
High School	30%	50%	85%
High School GPA	Above 4.0	Above 3.5	Above 3.0
(converted to 4.00 scale)	30%	80%	95%
SAT Middle 50th Percentile Range		Verbal	Math
(includes ACT scores converted to SAT format)		575–675	600–675

ACTIVITIES AND ACCOMPLISHMENTS

Varsity Letter	84%
Sports Team Captain	60%
Student Council or Club Officer	49%
Band/Chorus Member	30%

Table A-4. United States Merchant Marine Academy Class Profile

ACADEMICS (93% rank in the top 40% of their high school class)

Class Rank	Top 10%	Second 10%	Third and Fourth 10%
Class of 2018	35%	23%	35%

SAT Scores	Critical Reading	Math	Total
Class of 2018	632	652	1284
Average 2007–2017	600	626	1226

Table A-5. United States Air Force Academy Class Profile

TEST SCORES

SAT Verbal	SAT Math	ACT English	ACT Reading	ACT Math	ACT Science Reasoning
642	669	30.0	30.4	30.3	29.8

CANDIDATE FITNESS ASSESSMENT (CFA) Physical Profile

Exercise	Average for Men	Average for Women
Basketball Throw	70'	42'
Pull-Ups	12	3
Flexed-Arm Hang (Women)		24 sec.
Shuttle Run	8.4 sec.	9.5 sec.
Modified Sit-Ups (Crunches)	81	81
Push-Ups	63	43
One-Mile Run	6:12	7:03

Character Preparation and Leadership Profile

Activity	% of Class
Athletic Letter	79%
National Honor Society	69%
Scouting	23%
Class President/VP	18%
Boys/Girls State or Nation	17%
Valedictorian/Salutatorian	11%

Appendix III

Resources

INFORMATION ABOUT ACADEMIC HONOR SOCIETIES

There are many ways in which you can earn recognition for your academic accomplishments. Some reward general excellence, but others focus on specific topics, and still others are aimed at a particular state or geographic region. Here are some national honor societies along with website links.

You can only qualify for some honor societies by having grades or achievements above a certain level, but you can just join others. Notice that there are often additional award levels, contests, and even scholarships for which you might be qualified.

You can join some honor societies directly, but others require your school to have a local chapter that admits members. If your school doesn't have a chapter of the honorary society you're interested in, talk to your teachers in that subject to see what can be done.

SPECIAL NOTE! You may be notified that you've been selected for inclusion in a "Who's Who"–type book. Although listings are often free, you'll be asked to buy a copy of the book along with other memorabilia. At least some of these "Who's Who"–type books are simply scams, and there's evidence that college admissions officers in general don't give a lot of credence to such listings. Be careful and conduct due diligence before accepting the "honor."

General Academic Achievement

National Honor Society. Membership based on scholarship, leadership, service, and character. Chapters in many public schools (www.nhs.us).

Cum Laude Society. Similar to Phi Beta Kappa, but for secondary schools. Chapters primarily in private or independent schools (www.cumlaudesociety.org).

National Beta Club. General academic honors with a strong emphasis on community service (www.betaclub.org).

Specific Academic Areas

Delta Epsilon Phi. National honor society for high school students of German (www.aatg.org).

International Thespian Society. Student honorary organization for theater students in high school and middle school (www.schoolthe atre.org/ITS).

Mu Alpha Theta. National high school and two-year college mathematics honor society (www.mualphatheta.org).

National Art Honor Society. Recognizes high school students in grades 10–12 who have shown an outstanding ability in art (www.arteducators.org/community/nahs).

National Speech & Debate Association/National Forensic League. For students ranging from middle school through college (www.speechanddebate.org).

Quill and Scroll. International high school journalism honor societies, with chapters in over fourteen thousand high schools (http://quillandscroll.org).

Science National Honor Society. Encourages and recognizes high school students in the sciences (www.sciencenhs.org).

Société Honoraire de Français. National honor society that recognizes high school students who have maintained excellent grades in at least three semesters of French (www.frenchteachers.org/shf/).

Sociedad Honoraria Hispánica. Academic honor society for high school students studying Spanish (http://sociedadhonorariahispanica.net).

Tri-M Music Honor Society. Recognizes students for academic and musical achievements, with over six thousand chapters (www.nafme.org/programs/tri-m-music-honor-society/).

RESOURCES ABOUT LIFE AT MILITARY ACADEMIES

There are many fine books and other resources about life at military academies. Here are a few you may find of interest.

Cruikshank, Jeffrey L., and Chloe G. Kline. *In Peace and War: A History of the U.S. Merchant Marine Academy at Kings Point*. Hoboken, NJ: John Wiley & Sons, 2007.

Dwyer, Gail O'Sullivan. *Tough as Nails: One Woman's Journey through West Point*. Missoula, MT: Hellgate Press, 2009.

Fleming, Bruce. *Annapolis Autumn: Life, Death, and Literature at the U.S. Naval Academy*. New York: New Press, 2005.

Lipsky, David. *Absolutely American: Four Years at West Point*. New York: Vintage, 2004.

Schemo, Diana Jean. *Skies to Conquer: A Year Inside the Air Force Academy*. Hoboken, NJ: John Wiley & Sons, 2010.

Starr, Markham. *Swab Summer: Transformation at the United States Coast Guard Academy*. North Stonington, CT: Fowler Road Press, 2013.

Surviving West Point. (2003). DVD. West Point, New York: National Geographic.

The U.S. Naval Academy Class of 2002 [Joshua Welle, John Ennis, Katherine Kranz, and Graham Plaster]. *In the Shadow of Greatness: Voices of Leadership, Sacrifice, and Service from America's Longest War*. Annapolis, MD: Naval Institute Press, 2012.

Webb, James. *A Sense of Honor: A Novel*. Annapolis, MD: Naval Institute Press, 1995.

Year in the Blue: Inside the Air Force Academy. (2014). DVD. Colorado Springs, CO: Alan Hayden (director), Passion River Studio.

RESOURCES FOR TIME MANAGEMENT AND STUDYING FOR STUDENTS

Newport, Cal. *How to Become a Straight-A Student: The Unconventional Strategies Real College Students Use to Score High While Studying Less*. New York: Broadway Books, 2007.

Robinson, Adam. *What Smart Students Know: Maximum Grades, Optimum Learning, Minimum Time*. New York: Crown Trade Paperbacks, 1993.

RESOURCES FOR WRITING COLLEGE ESSAYS AND HANDLING INTERVIEWS

Bauld, Harry. *On Writing the College Application Essay, 25th Anniversary Edition: The Key to Acceptance at the College of Your Choice*. New York: HarperCollins, 2012.

Gelb, Alan. *Conquering the College Admissions Essay in 10 Steps: Crafting a Winning Personal Statement*, 2nd ed. Berkeley, CA: Ten Speed Press, 2013.

Metcalf, Linda. *How to Say It® to Get Into the College of Your Choice: Application, Essay, and Interview Strategies to Get You the Big Envelope*. New York: Prentice Hall, 2007.

INFORMATION ABOUT RELIGION AT THE ACADEMIES

West Point Office of Chaplains: http://www.usma.edu/chaplain/SitePages/
Home.aspx
US Naval Academy Chaplain's Center: http://www.usna.edu/Chaplains/
US Coast Guard Academy Command Religious Program: http://www.cga.edu/
cadet.aspx?id=437
US Merchant Marine Academy Spiritual Life: http://www.usmma.edu/acad
emy-life/activitiesservices/spiritual-life
US Air Force Academy Cadet Chaplain Corps: http://www.usafa.af.mil/units/
superintendent/usafa_hc/

Branum, Don. "Academy Chapel to Add Outdoor Circle to Worship Areas."
U. S. Air Force Academy. January 26, 2010. Accessed March 3, 2015. http://
www.usafa.af.mil/news/story.asp?id=123187157.
Carroll, Chris. "Atheists Groups Find Doors Open to Them at Service Academies." *Stars and Stripes*. August 24, 2011. Accessed March 3, 2015. http://
www.stripes.com/atheists-groups-find-doors-open-to-them-at-service-acad
emies-1.153110.
Kelleher, Elizabeth. "Military Academies Help Muslims Face Mecca." *IIP
Digital | U.S. Department of State*. November 21, 2006. Accessed March 3,
2015. http://iipdigital.usembassy.gov/st/english/article/2006/11/200611211
24320berehellek0.8676874.html#axzz3TMim18mb.
Rubin, Debra. "Campus Life 205: Yes, There Is Jewish Life at a Military
Academy." *Reform Judaism Online*. July 27, 2011. Accessed March 3, 2015.
http://reformjudaismmag.net/2011-Fall/RJ_57_Fall11.pdf.

RESOURCES FOR PREPARING FOR THE CANDIDATE
FITNESS ASSESSMENT

Smith, Stew. "How to Pass the Service Academy CFA." *Military.com*. Ac-
cessed March 9, 2015. http://www.military.com/military-fitness/fitness
-test-prep/service-academy-cfa.
Smothermom, Jordan. "Service Academy Candidate Fitness Assessment (CFA)
Basketball Throw Technique." *YouTube* (Strong Swift Durable Channel).
December 23, 2014. Accessed March 9, 2015. https://www.youtube.com/
watch?v=4LiaGbtE_Ao.
Smothermom, Jordan. "Service Academy Candidate Fitness Assessment
(CFA) Pull-Up Technique." *YouTube* (Strong Swift Durable Channel).
December 23, 2014. Accessed March 9, 2015. https://www.youtube.com/
watch?v=D9rHmwWkDnI.
Smothermom, Jordan. "Service Academy Candidate Fitness Assessment
(CFA) Push-Up Technique." *YouTube* (Strong Swift Durable Channel).
December 23, 2014. Accessed March 9, 2015. https://www.youtube.com/
watch?v=AUVCkVwDLTw.

Smothermom, Jordan. "Service Academy Candidate Fitness Assessment (CFA) Shuttle Technique." *YouTube* (Strong Swift Durable Channel). December 23, 2014. Accessed March 9, 2015. https://www.youtube.com/watch?v=Nns35rbgMNo.

USMA Admissions. "The West Point Candidate Fitness Assessment (CFA) Test." *YouTube*. August 26, 2014. Accessed March 9, 2015. https://www.youtube.com/watch?v=AlIZz9O7QiQ.

INFORMATION FOR PARENTS

Directorate of Admissions. "Information for New Cadets and Parents (Class of 2018)." United States Military Academy. Accessed March 26, 2015. http://www.usma.edu/parents/SiteAssets/Info-4-New-Cadets_Class-of-18.pdf.

Joiner, Lisa Browne, and Deborah L. W. Roszel. *The Mom's Guide to Surviving West Point*. Durham, NC: Torchflame Books, 2012.

Mackenzie, Ross H. *Brief Points: An Almanac for Parents and Friends of U.S. Naval Academy Midshipmen*. 3rd ed. Annapolis, MD: Naval Institute Press, 2004.

REPORTING FOR DUTY

Usually, new videos are uploaded for each incoming class. At the time of writing, the Class of 2018 was the most recent available. In some cases, I've listed earlier class videos because they were longer and more detailed. You can find a number of these videos for each academy, and more are uploaded each year.

While you're at it, look for other videos on different aspects of academy life. It's a good way to get an inside look at the institution you're trying to join.

Coast Guard Academy. "R-Day 2014: CGA Academy Life." YouTube. July 1, 2014. Accessed March 26, 2015. https://www.youtube.com/watch?v=UdZK-7e3S_U.

MileHiGuy51. "Air Force Academy Class of 2015 Reports for Duty." YouTube. June 30, 2011. Accessed March 26, 2015. https://www.youtube.com/watch?v=gKX4WPs2cXY.

USMMA AAF. "2014 U.S. Merchant Marine Academy Indoctrination." YouTube. July 2, 2014. Accessed March 26, 2015. https://www.youtube.com/watch?v=n-0Ah4beba4.

USNA AAF. "USNA's I-Day, Class of 2018." YouTube. August 4, 2014. Accessed March 26, 2015. https://www.youtube.com/watch?v=e4mV6BzhWec.

West Point Association of Graduates. "USMA Class of 2018 Reception Day." YouTube. July 9, 2014. Accessed March 26, 2015. https://www.youtube.com/watch?v=dknQ_qxxr28.

Appendix IV

Presidential Nomination Letters

To apply for a presidential service-connected or military-related nomination, you must send a letter to your academy. The academies provide sample letters on their respective websites, which are reprinted here.

WEST POINT

West Point uses the term "Service Connected Nomination" for presidential nominations:

http://www.usma.edu/admissions/Shared%20Documents/Service_Connected_Nomination_Sample.pdf.

Must reach West Point by JANUARY 31 of the year seeking admission

Date _____

Director of Admissions

United States Military Academy

West Point, New York 10996-1797

Dear Sir:

I request a nomination under the _____ category for the class entering the United States Military Academy in the Summer of 20___, and I submit the following data:

Name of Applicant: _____

Address: _____

Telephone Number: _____

Date of Birth: _____

Social Security Number: _____

Names of Parents: _____

Military Rank of Parent: _____

Social Security Number of Parent: _____

Component and Branch of Service of Parent: _____

Sincerely,

[Your Name]

NAVAL ACADEMY

The Naval Academy uses the term "Military-Affiliated Nomination" for presidential nominations:

http://www.usna.edu/Admissions/_files/documents/preslett.pdf.

This nomination request should be submitted after July 1 of the year prior to admission, and before January 31 of the year of admission.

Please Note: This nomination is for the natural or adopted children of active duty, reserve, or retired military parents ONLY

Office of Admissions Halsey Field House
ATTN: Nominations and Appointments Office
52 King George Street
Annapolis, MD 21402

Date: _____

Dear Sir:

I request a Presidential nomination to the United States Naval Academy for the class that will enter in June 20__, and I submit the following data:

Name: _____
(Give full name as shown on birth certificate or, if changed, attach copy of court order)

Address: (use ZIP code plus 4 and provide phone number)

Mailing: _____

Sex: M / F   Date of birth: _____

Name and address of high school/college: _____

Graduation: _____

Permanent: _____

Telephone: _____

Congressional state and district: _____

Applying to Senators and Congressmen (names):

_____

_____

_____

(month/year)

Candidate Number (Required): _____

If member of military, check here _____

Command: _____

Rate: _____ Branch of Service: _____ Duty Status:_____

You must have active duty, reserve or retired military PARENTS to qualify for this nomination. Your military service may qualify you for a Secretary of the Navy nomination, see your Command Career Counselor for details.

Information concerning parents' military service:

Name and rank of qualifying parent/s:

_____

Branch of Service: _____ Duty Status: _____

Command: _____

I verify that I have included the proper supporting documentation of my parent's military status with this application (check appropriate box):

- Active duty officers: statement of service signed by personnel officer specifying all periods of active duty.
- Active duty enlisted: statement of service prepared by personnel officer specifying all periods of active duty and listing dates of enlistment and dates of expiration of enlistment.
- Reserves: proof of current service, including a copy of most current annual statement of reserve points (minimum points required 2880) and valid identification card, or notice of eligibility (NOE) for retirement.
- Retired with pay: copy of DD Form 214 (Member's Copy 4)
- Deceased or 100% disabled: Veterans Administration official determination of 100% disability or service- connected death.

Sincerely yours,

(Signature)
Name

AIR FORCE ACADEMY

The Air Force Academy uses the term "Military-Affiliated Nomination" for presidential nominations:

http://www.academyadmissions.com/wp-content/uploads/2012/05/ReqMilitaryNom.pdf.

FORMAT OF REQUEST FOR MILITARY-AFFILIATED NOMINATION

(Use this format for any of these categories: Presidential, Children of Deceased or Disabled Veterans, or Children of Medal of Honor Recipients.)

HQ USAFA/RRS,
2304 Cadet Dr., Suite 2400
USAF Academy, CO 80840-5025

Dear Chief, Selections Division:
    I want to attend the Air Force Academy and to serve in the United States Air Force. I request a nomination under (the name of appropriate category) for the class that enters the Academy in June 20__.
    My pertinent data is:

Name (print name exactly as it appears on the birth certificate, or if legally changed, attach a copy of the court order):

Social Security Number:

Permanent address (street, city, county, state, zip code):

Temporary address (if applicable):

Permanent phone number and area code:

Temporary phone number and area code (if applicable):

Date and place of birth (spell out month):

If member of military, include rank, regular or reserve component, branch of service, and organizational address including PSC Box Number:

If previous candidate, indicate year:

Parental information - name, rank, social security number, component and branch of service:

If your parent is on active duty, attach a statement of service dated and signed by current personnel officer specifying all periods of active duty and any breaks therein. If your parent is in the Air Force they can access a statement of service online at their virtual MPF. If your parent is retired, attach a copy of the DD 214 (member copy 4), or retirement orders. If your parent is deceased attach a copy of the casualty report. If your parent is disabled attach the Veterans Administration (VA) claim number and VA office where the case is filed. If your parent is retired or deceased, documents can also be accessed at http://www.archives.gov/veterans/military-service-records/ regardless of their branch of service. If parent is a reservist, attach a copy of the document that shows their total point's credit or a copy of their notice of eligibility letter that states they are eligible to receive retired pay upon reaching 60 years of age.

Sincerely,

/Signature/
Name

Notes

CHAPTER 1. ABOUT THE ACADEMIES

1. "Top Public Schools (National Liberal Arts College)." *U.S. News and World Report, Education Rankings and Advice.* Accessed March 30, 2015. http://colleges.usnews.rankingsandreviews.com/best-colleges/rankings/national-liberal-arts-colleges/top-public.

CHAPTER 2. IS A SERVICE ACADEMY RIGHT FOR YOU?

1. Dobson, Michael, Paul Componation, Ted Leemann, and Scott P. Hutchins. 2009. "Decision Making," in *Applied Space Systems Engineering: Space Technology Series*, 1st ed., 201–32. Boston: McGraw Hill Learning Solutions.

CHAPTER 3. GETTING READY TO APPLY

1. "The SAT vs. the ACT." *The Princeton Review* (website). Accessed January 25, 2015. http://www.princetonreview.com/college/sat-act.
2. "*MacArthur*: The Film and More, Enhanced Transcript. Part One: Destiny." *American Experience*, PBS. Accessed January 25, 2015. http://www.pbs.org/wgbh/amex/macarthur/filmmore/transcript/transcript1.html.
3. Schalch, Kathleen. "Project Backpack: Children Help Katrina Victims." NPR. September 7, 2005. Accessed January 27, 2015. http://www.npr.org/templates/story/story.php?storyId=4835848.

CHAPTER 4. THE APPLICATIONS PROCESS

1. "Academic Performance." Air Force Academy. Accessed January 26, 2015. http://www.academyadmissions.com/admissions/the-application-pro cess/academic-performance/.
2. "Sample High School Profile." College Board, Accessed March 23, 2015. https://professionals.collegeboard.com/guidance/counseling/profile/sample.

CHAPTER 5. GETTING A NOMINATION

1. Korte, Gregory, and Fredreka Schouten. "Pride and Patronage: How Members of Congress Use a Little-Known Power to Shape the Military and Help Their Constituents." *USA Today*. September 16, 2014. Accessed February 17, 2015. http://www.usatoday.com/story/news/politics/2014/09/15/service-academies-congress-nomination-army-navy/15452669/.
2. Shesgreen, Deirdre. "How Lawmakers Dole Out Military Academy Nominations." Cincinnati.com (*The Cincinnati Enquirer*). September 15, 2014. Accessed February 18, 2015. http://www.cincinnati.com/story/news/politics/2014/09/15/cincinnati-lawmakers-military-academy-nominations/15676345/.

CHAPTER 6. SPECIAL ISSUES AND CONCERNS

1. Atkinson, Rick. *The Long Gray Line: The American Journey of West Point's Class of 1966*. Boston: Houghton Mifflin, 1989. 2829.
2. Goodstein, Laurie. "Air Force Academy Staff Found Promoting Religion." *The New York Times*. June 22, 2005. Accessed March 3, 2015. http://www.nytimes.com/2005/06/23/politics/23academy.html?pagewanted=all&_r=0.

CHAPTER 7. CANDIDATE FITNESS ASSESSMENT AND MEDICAL CLEARANCE

1. James, Alexa. "West Point Struggles to Fill Ranks." *Times-Herald Record (recordonline.com)*. February 26, 2009. Accessed March 9, 2015. http://www.recordonline.com/article/20090226/News/902260341.
2. Stanley, Clifford L. "Medical Standards for Appointment, Enlistment, or Induction in the Military Services (DoDI 6130.03)." Defense Technical Information Center (DTIC Online). September 13, 2011. Accessed March 10, 2015. http://www.dtic.mil/whs/directives/corres/pdf/613003p.pdf.

CHAPTER 8. ACCEPTANCES AND REJECTIONS

1. "Frequently Asked Questions—Early Action." United States Coast Guard Academy Admissions. Accessed March 24, 2015. http://www.cga.edu/admissions2.aspx?id=315. "Steps to Admissions: The West Point Application Process." West Point Admissions. Accessed March 24, 2015. http://www.usma.edu/admissions/SitePages/Steps.aspx.

2. "Online Viewbook." United States Naval Academy, Admissions. Accessed March 24, 2015. http://www.usna.edu/Viewbook/.

3. "Admissions." United States Merchant Marine Academy, page 6. Accessed March 24, 2015. http://www.usmma.edu/admissions.

4. "Steps to Admissions: The West Point Application Process." West Point Admissions. Accessed March 24, 2015.

5. Gasdoc. "USAF Academy Admissions Process." College Confidential. November 2, 2011. Accessed March 24, 2015. http://talk.collegeconfidential.com/air-force-academy-colorado-springs/1236212-usaf-academy-admissions-process.html.

6. Curtis, Rick. "Outdoor Action Guide to High Altitude: Acclimatization and Illnesses." Princeton University. Accessed March 26, 2015. http://www.princeton.edu/~oa/safety/altitude.html.

7. Ehrlich, Larry G. "The Power of First Encounters." In *Fatal Words and Friendly Faces: Interpersonal Communication in the Twenty-first Century*, 1821. Lanham, MD: University Press of America, 2000.

Bibliography

"Academic Performance | Air Force Academy." Air Force Academy. Accessed January 26, 2015. http://www.academyadmissions.com/admissions/the -application-process/academic-performance/.

"Admissions." United States Merchant Marine Academy. Accessed March 24, 2015. http://www.usmma.edu/sites/usmma.edu/files/docs/2014 USMMA Catalog Part 6-Adm.pdf.

Atkinson, Rick. *The Long Gray Line: The American Journey of West Point's Class of 1966.* Boston: Houghton Mifflin, 1989.

Curtis, Rick. "OA Guide to High Altitude: Acclimatization and Illnesses." Princeton University. Accessed March 26, 2015. http://www.princeton .edu/~oa/safety/altitude.shtml

Dobson, Michael, Paul Componation, Ted Leemann, and Scott P. Hutchins. 2009. "Decision Making." In *Applied Space Systems Engineering: Space Technology Series*, 1st ed., 201–32. Boston: McGraw Hill Learning Solutions.

Ehrlich, Larry G. "The Power of First Encounters." In *Fatal Words and Friendly Faces: Interpersonal Communication in the Twenty-first Century*, 18–21. Lanham, MD: University Press of America, 2000.

"Frequently Asked Questions—Early Action," United States Coast Guard Academy Admissions. Accessed March 24, 2015. http://www.cga.edu/ad missions2.aspx?id=315.

Gasdoc. "USAF Academy Admissions Process." College Confidential. November 2, 2011. Accessed March 24, 2015. http://talk.collegeconfidential.com/ air-force-academy-colorado-springs/123621wusaf-academy-admissions-pro cess.html.

Goodstein, Laurie. "Air Force Academy Staff Found Promoting Religion." *The New York Times.* June 22, 2005. Accessed March 3, 2015. http://www .nytimes.com/2005/06/23/politics/23academy.html?pagewanted=all&_r=0.

James, Alexa. "West Point Struggles to Fill Ranks." *Times-Herald Record (recordonline.com)*. February 26, 2009. Accessed March 9, 2015. http://www
.recordonline.com/article/20090226/News/902260341.

Korte, Gregory, and Fredreka Schouten. "Pride and Patronage: How Members of Congress Use a Little-Known Power to Shape the Military and Help Their Constituents." *USA Today*. September 16, 2014. Accessed February 17, 2015. http://www.usatoday.com/story/news/politics/2014/09/15/service
-academies-congress-nomination-army-navy/15452669/.

"MacArthur: The Film and More, Enhanced Transcript. Part One: Destiny." *American Experience*, PBS. Accessed January 25, 2015. http://www.pbs.org/
wgbh/amex/macarthur/filmmore/transcript/transcript1.html.

"Online Viewbook." United States Naval Academy, Admissions. Accessed March 24, 2015. http://www.usna.edu/Viewbook/admissions.php.

"Sample High School Profile." College Board, "For Professionals" Accessed March 23, 2015. https://professionals.collegeboard.com/guidance/counseling/
profile/sample.

"The SAT vs. the ACT." *The Princeton Review* (website). Accessed January 25, 2015. http://www.princetonreview.com/sat-act.aspx.

Schalch, Kathleen. "Project Backpack: Children Help Katrina Victims." NPR. September 7, 2005. Accessed January 27, 2015. http://www.npr.org/tem
plates/story/story.php?storyId=4835848.

Shesgreen, Deirdre. "How Lawmakers Dole Out Military Academy Nominations." Cincinnati.com (*The Cincinnati Enquirer*). September 15, 2014. Accessed February 18, 2015. http://www.cincinnati.com/story/news/poli
tics/2014/09/15/cincinnati-lawmakers-military-academy-nominations/156
76345/?from=global&sessionKey=&autologin=.

Stanley, Clifford L. "Medical Standards for Appointment, Enlistment, or Induction in the Military Services (DoDI 6130.03)." Defense Technical Information Center (DTIC Online). September 13, 2011. Accessed March 10, 2015. http://www.dtic.mil/whs/directives/corres/pdf/613003p.pdf.

"Steps to the West Point Application Process," West Point Admissions. Accessed March 24, 2015. http://www.usma.edu/admissions/SitePages/Steps
.aspx.

"Top Public Schools (National Liberal Arts College)." *U.S. News and World Report, Education Rankings and Advice*. Accessed March 30, 2015. http://
colleges.usnews.rankingsandreviews.com/best-colleges/rankings/national
-liberal-arts-colleges/top-public.

Index

529 Plan. *See* College Savings Plan
6130.03. *See* DoDI 6130.03

Academic honors. *See* Honors, academic
Academy Admissions Partner (USCGA). *See* Academy liaison officer
Academy Introduction Mission (AIM) Summer Program (USCG). *See* Academy summer programs
Academy liaison officer, 15, 27, 48, 49, 50, 52, 55, 57, 58, 117
Academy review board, 77
Academy summer programs, xviii, 35, 48, 53, 58
Acceptance, xx, 63, 120, 121
ACT. *See* Standardized tests
Additional Service Duty Obligation (ADSO), 11, 15
ADHD/mood disorders. *See* Learning disabilities
Admissions, competitiveness, 2
Admissions events, 47
Admissions standards. *See* Basic requirements for admission
Admissions portal. *See* Candidate portal
Advanced Placement (AP), 26, 30
Affidavit of residence, 78

African-Americans, 88, 89. *See also* Diversity
Air Force Academy. *See* United States Air Force Academy
Air Force Institute of Technology, 11
Alcohol. *See* Drug and alcohol abuse
Allergies, 105, 107
Alternatives to military service academies, 18–19, 121
American Legion, 36
Application process: advantages to starting early, 21–22; Air Force Academy, 58–60; Coast Guard Academy, 55–56; completion of, 117; earliest you can begin to apply, 21, 45; incomplete files, closing of, 118, 120; links to application websites, 45; Merchant Marine Academy, 56–57; Naval Academy, 53–55; notifications, 120; preliminary, 47, 53, 58; reapplying, 122; starting later, 22–23; West Point, 47–53
Appointment, 65, 120
Apps, cell phone and tablet, 46, 47
Arnold, Benedict, 3
Asthma, 86, 107
Athletics, 24, 62; highlight videos of, 85; honors and awards, 31,

62; leadership roles, 24, 62; not affiliated with schools, 31; recruitment of. *See* Recruited athletes

Balancing competing demands. *See* Time management
Bank account, 123
Basic requirements for admission, 14, 134, 142, 150, 155; Coast Guard additional requirements, 14
Beast Barracks, xx
Big Fat Envelope (BFE). *See* Acceptance
Blue and Gold Officer. *See* Academy liaison officers
Body modifications, 109, 110
Boys/Girls State, xviii, 36
Bribery, 74

Candidate Fitness Assessment (CFA), xviii, 50, 52, 62, 86, 95, 96–102, 118; benchmarks, 96; eligible administrators, 97; individual events, 98–102; test site, 98; videos, 97, 168–169
Candidate portal, 45, 48, 49, 63, 82, 110, 117, 121
CFA. *See* Candidate Fitness Assessment (CFA)
Charities, 39
Children of active duty or retired military. *See* Presidential nominations
Children of Medal of Honor winners. *See* Presidential nominations
Children of wounded, killed, or missing veterans. *See* Presidential nominations
Churches. *See* Religion
Citadel, The, 10
Citizenship, 14, 83, 91
Civil Air Patrol (CAP), 37
Class rank, 24, 26, 27, 61
Class profiles, 24
Clubs, school, 31, 33, 34

Coast Guard Academy. *See* United States Coast Guard Academy
College courses (non-Academy), 42
College rankings, 1
College Savings Plan (529 Plan), 124
Color blindness, 86, 108
Community colleges, 28, 42
Community influence, 62
Community service, 24, 39; with churches or religious groups, 39; with local or state government, 39; required for high school graduation, 39
Concussions, 86, 105, 108
Congressional nominations. *See* Nominations
Continuing education, 42
Conyers, John, 88
Course load, 15
Coursework, high school, 28
Creativity, 43
Current military or reserve nominations. *See* Nominations

Daily schedule for Academy students, 15
Dating, 16
Deadlines, 118
Debating, 32
Demerits and punishments, 16
Dental issues, 105, 110
Department of Defense Medical Review Board (DoDMERB), xviii, 52, 86, 95, 102–115, 117, 118, 120, 123; administrative remedial, 103, 111, 117; disqualified rating, 102, 105, 111; information and resources, 115; medical remedial, 103, 111, 117; problems after the examination, 112; process, 110–112; qualified rating, 102, 103, 111; rebuttal, 103, 104, 105, 112, 113; waiver, 104, 112, 113, 114–115, 118; website instructions, 105, 110
Disadvantaged applicants. *See* Hardship

Diversity candidates, 46, 88–89
DoDI 6130.03 (medical standards),
    105
DoDMERB. *See* Department of
    Defense Medical Review Board
    (DoDMERB)
Doubts, 13
Dramatics, 32
Drug and alcohol abuse, 59–60, 83,
    93, 109, 123
Drug and Alcohol Abuse Certificate
    (AF Form 2030), 59–60
Dual citizenship. *See* Citizenship
Dyslexia. *See* Learning disabilities

Eagle Scout, 24, 37
Early Action, 55, 119
Early Decision, 119
Economically disadvantaged. *See*
    Hardship
Eisenhower, Dwight D., 32, 33
Emergency Medical Technician
    (EMT), xviii, 40
Employer's evaluation. *See*
    References
Enlistment, 121
Environmentalism, 40
Essays, 41, 51, 57, 78–79, 167
Extracurricular activities, xviii, 31
Evaluation process, 23, 60; use of
    point system, 24–25, 60

Field Force Representative. *See*
    Academy liaison officer
Firefighting, volunteer, xviii, 40
Flippin, Henry O., 88
Force Field Analysis, 19
Foreign contacts, 123
Foreign students. *See* International
    students
Former cadets, 94

Georgia Military College (Coast
    Guard Academy Preparatory
    School), 10
Girls State. *See* Boys/Girls State

Glasses. *See* Vision issues
Goal-setting, 22
Gold Award Scout, 24, 37
Grades, xviii; after acceptance, 50–51;
    grade point average (GPA), 24,
    26; overcoming poor grades, 22;
    weighted and unweighted GPA, 26
Graduation rates, 14

Hair, 126
Hardship, 42, 83, 87–88
Hazing, 15
Head injuries. *See* Concussions
Height and weight standards, 106
Henriques, John, 6
Homeschooled applicants, 46, 62,
    83, 92–93; advice for, 92–93;
    pamphlet, 93
Honors, academic, 27
Honors courses, 26
Honor societies, 24, 27, 165–166
Hurricane Katrina, 40

Informational meetings, 77
Inhaler use, 86, 107
Initial deposit, 123
International Baccalaureate (IB)
    courses, 28
Interviewing, 79–82, 167; sample
    interview questions, 81–82
International students, 14, 73, 91,
    133–134, 141–142, 148–149, 154,
    157
Internships, 42

Journalism, student, 24
Junior Reserve Officers' Training
    Corps (JROTC), 37; Honor Units
    With Distinction, 38, 70

KISS ("Keep it simple, stupid!"), 79
Kościuszko, Tadeusz, 3

Lasik, 108
Law enforcement, encounters with,
    93–94

Leadership experience, 24
Learning disabilities, 86, 107, 108
Letter of Assurance (LOA), 118
Letter of Encouragement (LOE), 118
LGBT (Lesbian, Gay, Bisexual, Trans), 83, 90–91
Life at military service academies, 13–20, 166–167. *See also* Menninger Morale Curve
Local Admissions Field Reps (USMMA). *See* Academy liaison officers

MacArthur, Douglas, 4, 17, 32, 33
Marijuana. *See* Drug and alcohol abuse
Marion Military Institute (Coast Guard Academy Preparatory School), 10
McDonald, Deborah, 93, 95
McIntyre, Gene, 84
Measurement, 24
Medal of Honor. *See* Presidential nominations
Medical clearance. *See* Department of Defense Medical Review Board (DoDMERB)
Medical school, 11
Medications, 86, 109
Menninger Morale Curve, 126–127
Menninger, W. Walter, 126
Mental health, 105, 108
Merchant Marine Academy. *See* United States Merchant Marine Academy
Military-affiliated nomination. *See* Presidential nominations
Military school, xvii, 38–39; JROTC availability, 38
Military service academy. *See* Service academy
Morale. *See* Menninger Morale Curve

National Defense Intelligence College, 11
National Guard, 22, 121

National Letter of Intent (NLI), 119
National Merit Scholarship Qualifying Test (NMSQT). *See* Standardized tests
National waiting list, 72
Naval Academy. *See* United States Naval Academy
Naval Postgraduate School, 11
New Mexico Military Institute (Merchant Marine Academy Preparatory School), 10
Nimitz, Chester, 12
Nominations, xviii, 23, 52, 65, 117, 120, 121, 122, 130–133, 137–141, 144–148, 155–156; current military or reserve nominations, 70; different meanings of word, 66; essays, 41; JROTC/ROTC "Honor Units With Distinction," 38, 70; members of Congress, 66, 76–82; Merchant Marine Academy. *See* United States Merchant Marine Academy; nominations for children of active duty, killed or wounded, missing, or Medal of Honor winning veterans. *See* Presidential nominations; politics in nominations process, 74–75; Presidential nominations. *See* Presidential nominations; qualified alternates nominations, 72; remaining vacancy nominations, 72; service secretary nominations, 72; US territories and overseas possessions, 67, 68; Vice Presidential nominations, 68
Norwich University, 10

Officer Candidate School (OCS), 19
Operation Backpack, 41
Outward Bound, 41
Overnight visit. *See* Visiting

Packing lists, 125
Panama Canal Zone, 74, 157

Paperwork, importance of staying organized, 46. *See also* Time management
Parents, 17, 125, 169
Peace Corps, 126
Peer leadership, 32, 33, 37
Perry, Matthew, 5
Personal Data Record (USAFA Form 146), 59
Photograph, 78
Physical fitness, 95, 124
Physical Fitness Examination (PFE), 56
Piercings. *See* Body modifications
Politics, 74–75
Portal. *See* Candidate portal
Post-graduate education, 11
Powell, Colin, 9
Preliminary application. *See* Application
Preliminary Scholastic Aptitude Test (PSAT). *See* Standardized tests
Preparatory school (prep school), 10, 52, 84, 88 (*See also* preparatory schools for each individual service academy)
Presidential nominations, 68; applications process for, 69; children of active duty or retired military, 70; children of Medal of Honor winners, 70; children of wounded, killed, or missing veterans, 69; different names for, 69; lack of Merchant Marine nominations, 69; sample letters, 171–176
Problems in school, 94. *See also* Trouble
Public speaking, 32

Qualified alternates, 71, 72

Ranked and unranked nominations, 66, 75, 77
R-Day. *See* Reporting for duty
Reapplying, 55, 122

Recruited athletes, 30, 83, 84–86, 119; academy athletic department contacts, 85
References, 51, 52, 54, 56, 57, 59, 62, 63, 117; preparing your references, 55, 59; potential reference problems, 54; submitting additional references, 55
Regimentation, 13, 15
Regional Commander (West Point). *See* Academy liaison officer
Regional Director (USNA). *See* Academy liaison officer
Religion: Air Force Academy scandal, 91; community service opportunities, 39; diversity, 91, 168; religious preference, 91, 168
Remaining vacancy nominations, 72
Reporting for duty, xx, 56, 125–126, 169
Requirements. *See* Basic requirements for admission
Revenue Cutter Service, 6
Reserve Officer Training Corps (ROTC), xvii, 9, 19, 22, 121; Honor Units With Distinction, 70
Rolling admissions, 120

Salary, 1, 2, 7, 123
Salutatorian. *See* Honors, academic
Scholarships, 124
Scholastic Aptitude Test (SAT). *See* Standardized tests
School profile, 62
Science, Technology, Engineering, Math (STEM), 33, 34, 35
Scouting, 24, 37, 62
Sea Cadets (US Naval Sea Cadet Corps), 37
Seasonal allergies. *See* Allergies
Security clearance, 46, 122–123
Self-assessment, 17
Senior Military Colleges, 9
Service academy: applying to multiple academies, 11; pros and cons, 18; right for you, 20; which one, 11, 12

Service-connected nominations. *See* Presidential nominations

Service obligation, 1, 13; if you leave the academy, 13; serving in a different branch of the military, 11

Service secretary nominations for qualified alternates, 72

Shoes and boots, 118, 123

Sports. *See* Athletics

Standardized tests, xviii, 28, 50, 78; submitting test scores, 29; superscoring, 29

Student government, 24, 32

Student publications, 33

Study habits, 25. *See also* Time management

Submitting additional information, 51

Suicide, 17. *See also* Mental health

Summer Leadership Experience (SLE). *See* Academy summer programs

Summer programs (non-Academy), 42

Summer Seminar (USNA, USAFA). *See* Academy summer programs

Summer STEM Program (USNA). *See* Academy summer programs

Superintendent's Nominations, 72, 86

Surgery, 86, 108, 109. *See also* Department of Defense Medical Review Board (DoDMERB)

Swab Summer. *See* Reporting for duty

Tattoos. *See* Body modifications

Teacher evaluations. *See* References

Texas A&M University, 10

Thayer, Silvanus, 3

Time management, 25, 26, 167

Transcripts, 50, 117

Travel, 41, 42, 43, 125

Trouble, 83, 93–94, 123

Tuition, 1, 13

Tutoring, 34

T/V *Kings Pointer*, 8

Uniformed Services University of the Health Sciences, 11

United States Air Force Academy, 9, 120; applications process, 58–60; authorized strength, 144; class profile, 164; laws governing appointments, 144–152

United States Air Force Academy Preparatory School, 10

United States Army Command and General Staff College, 11

United States Coast Guard Academy, 5, 119, 120; authorized strength, 152; class profile, 163; no nominations required, 6, 65; laws governing appointments, 152–154

United States Coast Guard Academy preparatory school. *See* Georgia Military College and Marion Military Institute

United States Life-Saving Service, 6

United States Military Academy (West Point), 3, 120; applications process, 47–53; authorized strength, 129; class profile, 162; laws governing appointments, 129–136

United States Military Academy Preparatory School, 10, 52

United States Merchant Marine Academy, 120; applications process, 45, 56–57; class profile, 164; costs of attendance, 7; differences in nomination process, 68, 73–74, 155–156; different service obligation requirements, 8; laws governing appointments, 154–160; no summer program, 35; non-military nature of, 7

United States Merchant Marine Academy Preparatory School. *See* New Mexico Military Institute

United States Naval Academy, 4, 120; applications process, 53–56; authorized strength, 137; class

profile, 163; laws governing
  appointments, 137–144
United States Naval Academy
  Preparatory School, 10
University of North Georgia, 10
Unranked nominations. *See* Ranked
  and unranked nominations
USA Today, 74, 75
USCGC *Eagle*, 6
US News and World Report, 1
USS *Somers*, mutiny, 5
US territories and overseas
  possessions. *See* Nominations

Valedictorian. *See* Honors, academic
Varsity letter, xviii, 24. *See also*
  Athletics
Veterans, children of. *See*
  Presidential nominations
Veterans, military, 40
Vice Presidential nominations. *See*
  Nominations
Virginia Military Institute, 10

Virginia Polytechnic Institute and
  State University (Virginia Tech),
  10
Vision issues, 23, 86, 105, 108, 110
Visiting, 13, 118
Volunteers In Service to America
  (VISTA), 126

Walt Whitman High School, 41
Weight. *See* Height and weight
  standards
Well-rounded, importance of, 23. *See
  also* Evaluation process
West Point. *See* United States
  Military Academy (West Point)
"Whole Person" evaluation process.
  See Evaluation process
Women, 90
Working, 42
Wounded Warriors (organization),
  40

Yearbook, 24

About the Author

Photo Credit: Humayun Mirza

Michael Singer Dobson is the author of over thirty books on topics ranging from project management to military history. A frequent keynote speaker and popular workshop leader, he has given well over one thousand presentations on three continents.

Dobson was part of the original team that built and opened the Smithsonian Institution's National Air and Space Museum on the Mall in Washington, DC. He worked as a career counselor and writer for the Résumé Place and contributed to several books on Federal employment. He was also head of game design and marketing for *Dungeons & Dragons®* publisher TSR Inc. He is a graduate of the University of North Carolina at Charlotte.

His bestselling book *Practical Project Management* has been called "the best project management book ever written." *Enlightened Office Politics*, coauthored with his wife Deborah Singer Dobson, was named one of the 100 Best Business Books of 2001 by the *Library Journal*. His novels *Fox on the Rhine* and *MacArthur's War* were both selections of the Military Book Club. His game *AD&D Battlesystem* won the prestigious H. G. Wells Award. His works have been translated into Chinese, German, and Polish.

In 2010, Dobson was awarded the Samaritan Medal for Peace and Humanitarian Service by the indigenous Samaritan people for his work in Israel and the West Bank. He is (as far as he knows) the world's only private owner of an Apollo spacesuit.

Dobson has lived in North Carolina, Germany, Alabama, Wisconsin, Illinois, and the Washington, DC, area. He is married to frequent coauthor Deborah Singer Dobson, a human resources executive. They have one son, James, who is a cadet at West Point, and two Shelties, who are not.

For more, visit http://militaryacademy.info.